PRAIRIE WINDS

Prairie Winds

Hilda Amanda Ericksen

To order additional copies of this book, contact:
Xlibris Corporation
1-888-7-XLIBRIS
www.Xlibris.com
Orders@Xlibris.com

CONTENTS

SHORT STORIES

In loving memory of my mother,

Lily Elvira Hanson

PROLOGUE

This book began as a collection of short stories and assignments for various writing classes I took through the Institute of Children's Literature. Eventually the book has become a reflection of my family, memories, and life with its many blessings and sorrows. Bringing the collections of memories and stories together as a published book represents one of my lifelong goals.

Many Minnesotans have been slow to adopt the cuisine of one of our largest cultures–the foods that our grandmother's brought from Sweden. These foods are a strong part of my family's heritage. As a Scandinavian, food is the common denominator throughout all of life's major (and minor) occurrences. Whether it's a baby shower, wedding, Christmas dinner, funeral, St. Lucia Day, or a family reunion–you can always count on Scandinavians to supply good food and LOTS of it. For these reasons I chose the topic of Scandinavian foods as one of my very first writing assignments, and why I have also chosen to include my favorite recipes throughout the book.

Ask anyone on the street, Scandinavian's included, to name some traditional Scandinavian foods. No doubt lutefisk, lefse, and herring will rank at the top. In fact, Scandinavian cuisine is much more diverse than Church suppers of lefse and lutefisk. It has been said the only things we Scandinavians will own up to, in the name of fellowship among our countries, are the Vikings. True enough, the Vikings are part of the common cultural heritage of Scandinavia, but they are by no means the only part. Ever since the earliest settlements in these lands, foods and customs have intermingled among the countries and blended with influences from foreign shores, which created a cuisine and a culture that take second to none. No one can approximate the age of a dish like herring salad, eaten for so many years and enjoyed so thoroughly not only in Scandinavia but wherever they had gone.

Sweden ranks second only to France in quality and quantity of cheese production. Of Sweden's legendary crispbreads, an average Swede consumes two slices a day. Swedes eat ten times more fish than Americans and seventy-five percent less red meat. Vegetables and fruit are also high in their diet. For many years the recipes being used today were not written but handed down mouth-to-mouth, memory-to-memory. Out of the north came one of the greatest delicacies, cured salmon, and their finest fish. It can be poached, broiled, baked, smoked or cured with salt, sugar, white pepper and dill. Scandinavian food is many things: fish of course, pork, poultry and moose as well as beets, potatoes, cucumbers, dill, parsley, horseradish, apples, almonds, cream, and golden butter. In short, it is cooking pure and simple.

I want to thank everyone—teachers, grandchildren and family—who helped make this book a reality. I hope you enjoy the following memories as much as I have enjoyed living them the past 87 years.

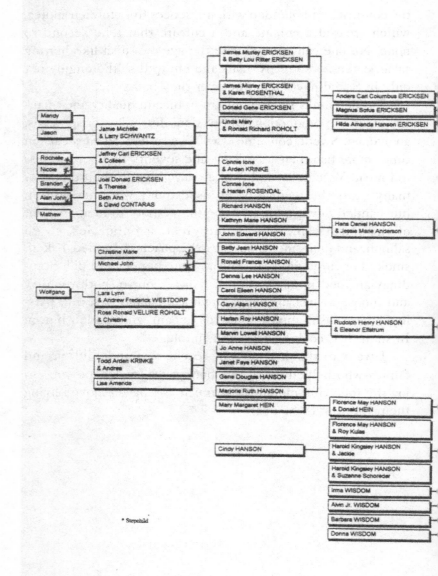

* Stepchild

The Family Tree

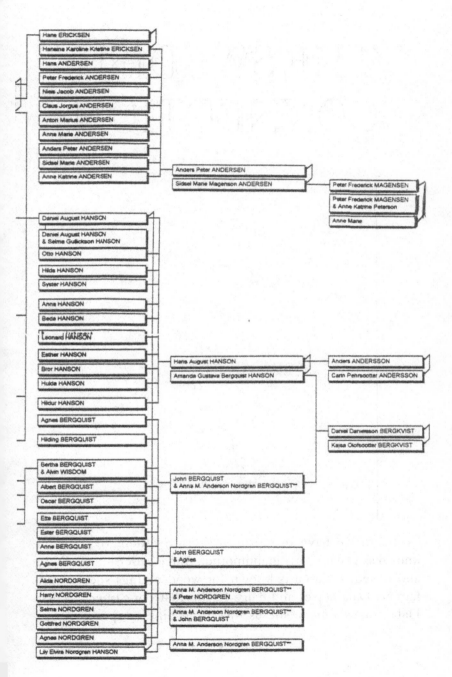

Hans ERICKSEN

Hansine Karoline Kristine ERICKSEN

Hans ANDERSEN

Peter Frederick ANDERSEN

Niels Jacob ANDERSEN

Claus Jorgus ANDERSEN

Anton Marius ANDERSEN

Anne Marie ANDERSEN

Anders Peter ANDERSEN

Sidsel Marie ANDERSEN

Anne Katrine ANDERSEN

Anders Peter ANDERSEN

Sidsel Marie Magensen ANDERSEN

Peter Frederick MAGENSEN

Peter Frederick MAGENSEN & Anne Katrine Peterson

Anne Marie

Daniel August HANSON

Daniel August HANSON & Selma Gullickson HANSON

Otto HANSON

Hilda HANSON

Syster HANSON

Anna HANSON

Beda HANSON

Leonard HANSON

Esther HANSON

Bror HANSON

Hulda HANSON

Hans August HANSON

Amanda Gustava Bergquist HANSON

Anders ANDERSSON

Carin Pehrsdotter ANDERSSON

Hildur HANSON

Agnes BERGQUIST

Hilding BERGQUIST

Daniel Danielsson BERGKVIST

Kajsa Olofsdotter BERGKVIST

Bertha BERGQUIST & Alvin WISDOM

Albert BERGQUIST

Oscar BERGQUIST

Etta BERGQUIST

Ester BERGQUIST

Anne BERGQUIST

Agnes BERGQUIST

John BERGQUIST & Anna M. Anderson Nordgren BERGQUIST***

John BERGQUIST & Agnes

Aida NORDGREN

Harry NORDGREN

Selma NORDGREN

Gottfred NORDGREN

Agnes NORDGREN

Lily Elvira Nordgren HANSON

Anna M. Anderson Nordgren BERGQUIST*** & Peter NORDGREN

Anna M. Anderson Nordgren BERGQUIST*** & John BERGQUIST

Anna M. Anderson Nordgren BERGQUIST***

THE SWEDISH CONNECTION

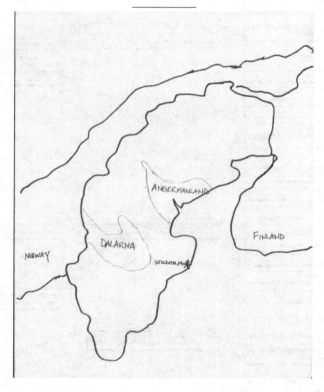

To begin we have to go to northern Sweden. In a region known as Dalarna, my grandmother, Anna Anderson, was born and raised. Dalarna is known for woodcarvings such as the famous Dala horses and dairy. In the 1840s or earlier the first Dala horses were made as toys from pine or spruce scraps left over from furniture makings. Dala painting is a style of wall painting, more than a century old, from the Dalarna province. It is especially wide spread in the towns of Rattoick, Leksand, and Mora. Kurbit leaves are a characteristic of Dalarna painting. In the book of Jonah, chapter four, the Kurbit, meaning plant or gourd, is a symbol of both vitality and death. Anna's dad, my great grandfather, was a furniture maker and Anna painted Dala horses he carved out of the scraps.

Early in her childhood Anna became quite deaf from a siege of red measles. This did not stop her from becoming a dairymaid. In the summer the dairymaid were shepherds, who moved the cattle up into the mountains. The cows were called with a long trumpet called a lur. A young dairymaid could call to her animals, or to people as a warning signal, and could be heard up to three miles. These dairymaid were also responsible for milking the cows, churning butter, and making cheese from the milk.

As a young woman Anna was quite beautiful. She had golden hair, sparkling blue eyes, a straight nose and full lips. While still in her teens she became acquainted with a traveling salesman. When she became pregnant by this salesman— her parents flatly refused to let her marry this commoner. Instead they bought her a ticket to America, because of the shame she had brought upon this proud couple. Did the prairie winds have something to do with her arriving in Brunswick, Minnesota, near Mora, or was it an act of fate that she came to this new strange land not knowing a soul?

Anna Nordgren Bergquist

She stayed in Brunswick for a short while. The store-keeper encouraged her to walk a couple of miles east of Brunswick to a farm that may be willing to exchange work for her board and room. She was hired at the farm and remained there until her pregnancy became noticeable, at which time she was asked to leave. "Whatever will I do?" she asked the couple. They told her of a bachelor living a mile west of their farm in the second house on the north side of the road. "Go and ask him to marry you. He is a very kind man, but much older than you. His name is Peter Nordgren. If he agrees, he will be a wonderful father to your baby."

Anna packed her few belongings and started walking towards Brunswick. It was winter and she was cold. As she walked she tried to figure out where she was going to find the courage to ask the stranger to marry her. "Could this really be any worse than being thrown out of my home in Sweden?" When she reached the second house on the right she noticed the house was a two-story, gingerbread home, with a columned open porch, painted white with many trees lining the driveway.

She was shaking from fear and the cold as she knocked at the door. The door opened and there was a blue eyed, five foot ten inch tall, thin man with a mustache asking her to enter. He greeted her in Swedish. She noticed his smile and kind looking face. In their conversations she told him about her life in Sweden, including being quite deaf and pregnant. She expanded on how well she could cook, bake, sew, milk cows, and make cheese. Peter shared that he had also come from Dalarna.

Anna noticed how sympathetic Peter was to her need— thus giving her the courage to ask him to marry her. He must of thought this young lady is still in her teens, but she can be a companion and I am lonely. He agreed to marry her. They were married in the parsonage at Brunswick by the Lutheran pastor.

Peter was known for his kindness and Anna was very happy there. He was so considerate of her condition and she enjoyed her new home. She made curtains and braided rugs. The white pine floor was scrubbed weekly. She knitted and crocheted things for the baby expected in August. Peter was gone most of the week. He worked on a large farm known as the Bronson Farm located west of Mora. He walked to work on Mondays and came home on Saturdays. It was twelve miles to walk one way. He was thankful for Anna. He purchased a few cows after she came and appreciated the homemade cheese, butter and bread. There was a light in the window and warm food waiting for his arrival each weekend.

When the time approached for her to give birth, Peter arranged for a midwife. On August 8, 1893, a baby girl was born. They named her Lily Elvira—this baby was my mother. Peter and Anna's family grew. Alida was born in 1895, Harry in 1896, Selma in 1898, and Gottfred in 1901. This was a very happy home where the children laughed and played, receiving much affection from both Anna and Peter.

Lily was adopted by Peter, given the surname of Nordgren, and raised as if she were his child. She attended school in Brunswick where she graduated from the eighth grade. She received her Christian education at the Baptist church across from the school. Her mother Anna was a devout Christian lady. She had ten years of having a gentle kind father, Peter.

Tragedy struck in 1902 when Alida died at the age of four from diphtheria. Double tragedy followed with the death of Peter in 1903 from tuberculosis. In 1905 Harry also died from Diphtheria. Gottfred died at sixteen from a ruptured appendix. Only Lily and Selma lived for many years. Anna knew what sorrow was, it never seemed to end. One wonders how much one person can bear—there seemed to be no end of mourning for Anna to endure. She had enjoyed such a happy life with Peter and their dear children. "Will this, heartsick part of my life ever end?" she cried. She was comforted in caring for her remaining children.

Peter Nordgren

Across the road from the sixty-acre farm owned by Peter Nordgren, was John Bergquist's forty-acre farm. John and his wife, Agnes, were happy for Peter when he married Anna. They became close friends and often visited back and forth. The Bergquist and Hanson families were also Swedish from the Angermanland region at Resele on the Angermanland River.

Angermanland is one of the northernmost provinces of Sweden, sharing its northern boundary with Lapland. Summer days are long and winter days short. This is the land of the midnight sun that embraces all of Sweden. Here in this northern land rich in pine and spruce forests, swift rivers carry logs to the paper mills. The chief export of this land is fish:

cod, herring and salmon. In the growing season wild berries such as lingonberries and cloudberries, to name a few, grow in abundance and are a delicacy. Angermanland is also noted for its fine linen weaving and handmade rugs that are made of worn out clothing.

John Bergquist immigrated to America in the 1870s or early 1880s. Real stout-hearted Swedes, for other reasons than poverty; immigrated to America with a firm determination to succeed. Success meant good food to eat. For the women, the enjoyment was having enough ingredients available to prepare the dishes they once only dreamt about. This put lightness in their steps from stove to table.

Could the prairie winds have intervened again? John Bergquist settled half a mile east of Brunswick, Minnesota. He married and had a large family. John's wife, Agnes, Anna's dear friend, also died in 1903 from pneumonia, the same year Peter passed away. Being friends, Anna and John consoled each other. They married in 1906. I never knew if theirs was a marriage of convenience, consolement or security. They lived in the Nordgren home, for this was the home Anna loved and would not leave.

In October 1908 Anna gave birth to Bertha, followed by Hilding two years later, then Agnes, who died in infancy. This Bergquist-Nordgren family in 1912 embraced John's seven, Anna's three living children, along with their own two. Most of John's children from his first marriage were on their own.

John was a tall, arrogant, proud, big boned man. He had dark hair, brown eyes and wore a mustache. He was not the gentleman that Peter Nordgren was. Not many words were spoken between he and Anna. Silently she would stand by the stove preparing the scanty meals; in silence she would place the food on the table thinking, "will there be enough to go around?" Saying grace before meals was now dropped. John and the children would spread themselves around the table—never any room for Anna. This was a carry over from

Sweden where the wife stood by the stove and served the family—this custom had not been observed in her former home with Peter. Meals for her in this marriage were eaten while walking or sitting by the edge of the stove. John enforced this custom from his life in Sweden. When food was short at times, it was not John who went with less. It did not bother him one bit to spread his bread with butter while the rest of the family used molasses or syrup.

He believed strongly that children were to be seen and not heard. Child rearing followed firm rules. It was customary to use the rod and the woodshed. Perhaps more cruel or far more lasting in effect was the way children were treated in general. Their feelings and budding aspirations were disregarded or treated with indifference; visible display of affection was not seen. From childhood they were taught to observe the rule of modesty, any sign of vanity was squelched. Consequently, he had a very well behaved family. After the children graduated from eighth grade, they left home. The boys either worked in lumber camps or for farmers. The girls worked in households as maids.

John was known as one of the strongest men in the area. It was said that he could drive a nail into wood with his bare hands and open a horseshoe. He displayed his skills at the Brunswick store. Contrary to the belief that Swedes were poor letter writers, John was a good correspondent. He often wrote to his relatives in Sweden telling them how well off he was and how much he loved this new land. He would often write to his sister, Amanda, in Sweden. Amanda was married to Daniel Hanson. To this union many children were born including August, Bror, Leonard, Otto, Hildur, Hilda, Esther, Beda, Sister and Anna. In John's letters he encouraged his nephews to immigrate to America. He was successful in getting three Hanson nephews to leave Sweden. Leonard went as far west as Montana, Otto landed in British Columbia, and August immigrated to Yellow Grass, Saskatchewan, Canada.

John had a strong interest in his nephew August, the eldest of the three brothers. He invited August to spend Christmas with his family in Minnesota in 1911. August was thrilled to be invited to his Uncle John's home and readily accepted.

Around the turn of the century, Daniel August Hanson, known as "Big August", left his homeland, Resele, Sweden and his family including his father Daniel, mother Amanda, six sisters and three brothers. He immigrated to Canada, North America. He eventually settled in Yellow Grass, Saskatchewan, a small town in the South Central part of the province. He got his name "Big August" by being the eldest and tallest of his nine sisters and brothers. He was a handsome, six-foot two-inch tall man with thick black hair, dark brown eyes and a black mustache. He stood as tall and straight as a Norway pine tree, in spite of surviving a dynamite explosion in Sweden during a road building accident in central Angermanland. He then survived thirty-five operations on the right side of his body leaving it noticeably smaller, especially his leg and arm. There was also some discoloration on the right side of his face but this did not distract from his handsomeness.

In all, he was quite talented. He sang, played the accordion, and in Sweden he had performed on the stage singing, playing the accordion and acting. He worked in construction and masonry. August was 25 years old when he arrived in Yellow Grass. In Yellow Grass he was a drayman, a self-employed man who met the trains each day with his horse drawn wagon to load and deliver supplies to businessmen. He supplemented this with construction.

Hilda and Amanda Hanson

Living with John Bergquist and his style of raising children was hard on Lily. Being the eldest stepdaughter, much was expected of her. At nineteen years of age, Lily had blossomed into a lovely young lady. She was slightly over five-foot tall, pleasingly formed with dark brown hair and blue eyes that sparkled when she smiled. Her peaches and cream complexion enhanced her off the face hairstyle loosely woven into a knot. She had many of her mother's characteristics of being soft-spoken, mild mannered, amiable and meek. Lily spoke and wrote Swedish fluently having been taught by Peter and Anna. As soon as she finished eighth grade she worked as a maid for a well-to-do family in Cambridge. She was working for this family at the time that August was expected to visit her stepfather and August's uncle, John Bergquist, in 1911.

Lily Elvira Nordgren Hanson

Unbelievable as it seemed a bonding between Scandinavia, Minnesota and Saskatchewan began in December 1911 when August visited his uncle in Brunswick, Minnesota escorted by the prairie winds.

Anna was excited about meeting August whom John referred to as "Big August". Some of the children would be coming home for Christmas to meet the guest from Canada, including Lily. Anna was very proud of her first born who had developed into a beautiful young lady. Anna secretly thought "maybe a romance can bloom between August and Lily."

Both Anna and John were excited about preparing and sharing a traditional Swedish Christmas including Lucia Day, Lucia buns, Julotta services on Christmas Day and gifts on Christmas Eve with dancing around the Christmas tree. John got busy butchering and Anna baked. She made the customary seven kinds of cookies and several kinds of breads.

The Santa Lucia celebration honors St. Lucia, the patron saint of light. The celebration is held each December thirteenth, which according to tradition is the day following the longest night of the year. The festival is a Swedish tradition in which the eldest daughter in the family rises early, and dons a white robe, crimson sash, and a crown of candles. The daughter then brings saffron buns, ginger cookies and coffee to members of the household in memory of St. Lucia distributing food during famines.

For Swedes, Christmas more than just another holiday, it was the time for sentiment and joy. Stored feelings came out in the open and the freedom to express what was in the heart was joyously embraced. These releases of emotions made for a warmer companionship and at no other time of the year are there such gratifying attachments formed as at Christmas. Formality was put on the shelf and the Christmas spirit took over. Most of the food was prepared early in the month so the Christmas season could be thoroughly enjoyed without stopping to prepare food. The days of scrubbing, baking and cooking terminated with Christmas Eve.

August arrived in mid-December. John was eager to introduce all that were there. "These are your first cousins," he said as he named them off, Albert, Oscar, Etta, Ester, Annie, and Agnes. "These are Anna's children, Lily, Selma and Gottfred Nordgren, your step cousins." They all, including August, eagerly joined in with the last preparations for Christmas. What a celebration they all had on Christmas Eve. After a sheaf of oats was put out for the birds and the cattle and horses were given an ample feeding of grain, the hours of feasting began. Aside from the usual array of herring and small boiled potatoes, was an omelet filled with creamed mushrooms, meatballs, platters of cold meat, roast pork loin with stewed prunes, veal roast, Doppigryta (dip in the pot) consisting of ham, potato and pork sausage and rolled meat boiled together. When the meat was removed from the kettle, everyone dipped bread in the hot broth. Dessert was a large torte and a red berry pudding called "Kram". All this food was washed down with "Glogg," a drink made of red wine, raisins, orange peel and spices, served hot.

Santa Claus would arrive with a jolly greeting of "Are there any good children here?" With the candle-lit tree pulled out into the center of the room, all would join hands and dance and sing around the tree. Gaily wrapped presents were unwrapped with much singing and chatter. True to Anna's dreaming, August and Lily took a keen interest in each other—a budding romance started. Lily noticed how tall and handsome he was. Soon they were standing side by side as more dancing and singing around the tree continued. August asked Lily to perform the actions to a song as a couple. She was very impressed about how light he was on his feet and how well he sang. Lily could see that he loved music as much as she. Being a singer he was asked to sing, which he did.

Gubben Noah, Gubben Noah, var en herdersman, Nar han gick ur arken, plantera pa marken, myket vin, ya mycket vin ya detta gjorde han. Ya, nu dr det jul igen.

Translation: Old man Noah, Old man Noah, was an honorable man, when he left the ark he planted in the ground vines, yes, many vines, yes this indeed he did. Yes, now it is Christmas again.

Anna announced, "It's time to eat again." This time the seven kinds of cookies, several kinds of bread, cheese, meats, and beet pickles; a regular smorgasbord.

SWEDISH MEATBALLS
1 pound ground beef
1 pound ground pork
2 tablespoons chopped onion
1 teaspoon butter
1 egg
1 tablespoon sugar
1 ½ teaspoon salt
½ teaspoon pepper
3 tablespoons dry bread crumbs
1 large potato mashed
2 tablespoons butter
4 tablespoons water

GRAVY
Drippings from meatballs
1 teaspoon flour
¾ cup half and half
¼ cup water
Salt to taste

Grind meats together twice. Sauté onion in 1 teaspoon of butter and let cool. Mix all ingredients except butter. Shape mixture into small balls. In a heavy 10 to 12 inch skillet, melt 2 tablespoons of butter over high heat. Reduce heat and brown balls on all sides, then cook for 6-10 minutes, or until there is no trace of pink inside of meat. Pour gravy over balls and serve.

SWEDISH KRAM
2 ½ cups grape juice (or any other juice)
¼ teaspoon salt
1 tablespoon lemon juice
½ cup sugar
¼ cup minute tapioca or cornstarch

Mix all ingredients and cook in a double boiler until the

mixture thickens. Pour into a serving bowl. Sprinkle with cinnamon and serve warm with cream or half and half.

PICKLED HERRING
3 to 4 large salted herring
1 cup vinegar
½ cup sugar
1 bay leaf crushed
1 teaspoon allspice
½ teaspoon mustard seeds
10 whole cloves
1 medium red onion thinly sliced
Clean herring and soak in cold water about 12 hours, changing the water at least twice. Cut herring diagonally into one-inch pieces. Boil vinegar and sugar together, then cool. Mix bay leaves, allspice, mustard seeds and whole cloves. In a glass jar, arrange some of the spice mixture, herring pieces and onion continue in layers. Pour the cooled vinegar mixture over the layers, cover and refrigerate at least 12 hours.

Before August returned to Yellow Grass he and Lily had gone on several walks and agreed to correspond. He was happy to have met all his first cousins and step cousins. Lily was no relation. August promised to return for Christmas in 1912. Winter, spring, summer, and fall came and went. Lily could hardly wait for the letters she received from August. All correspondence was written in Swedish. The closer to December it got, those letters diverted from friendly feelings to love.

August returned to Brunswick, Minnesota for another visit in early December 1912. He came with the intention of asking Lily to marry him. They got to know each other well by corresponding for a year. He truly felt she would say yes but still felt timid about asking her. Then it did happen. They were married on December 13, 1912 in Brunswick. The ceremony was simple, he wore his black suit and Lily wore an ivory satin dress that she had made with elbow length sleeves, an overlay skirt and an off the face full-length veil with ribbons and lace. She wore her watch, a decorative necklace and the opal ring August gave her as an engagement ring. They were a handsome couple and were very happy.

After Christmas August returned to Yellow Grass with his new bride. Prairie winds had invaded Sweden, Minnesota, and now had rotated back to Saskatchewan.

Lily and August Hanson's Wedding Picture

SASKATCHEWAN

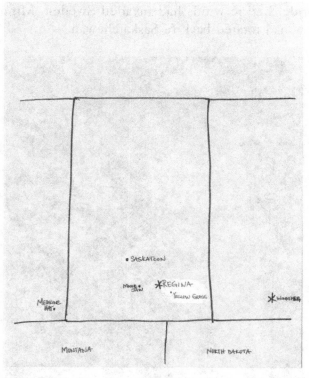

During the first part of the twentieth century pioneers swelled the land across Canada. World economics, cheap homestead lands and the coming of the trains all made rapid colonization of the prairies possible. Saskatchewan, Canada is a very special place; one of Canada's four western provinces, it covers more than a quarter million square miles. Half the province is covered by forest in the northern part, one third is improved farmland and one eighth is fresh water. At first the word was "Kisiskatchewan" named by the plain Indians, meaning the river that flows swiftly—the most important waterway running through this territory. Many of its people have roots in Europe: Russia, Poland, Scandinavia, and the British Isles.

There is a beauty here that transcends the lakes, the forests and the dazzling big sky sunsets. This beauty is a feeling, a sense of belonging, and a kinship with the land. This beauty is in her people, a warm and caring family's struggles and achievements. Hard work, cooperation and an abiding respect for the great powers of nature, especially the wind, controlled and contributed to the livelihood of its diverse nationalities.

The prairie winds blow over a hundred thousand fresh water lakes, clover, ripening wheat fields and miles of prairie. One can sense the magic of this province all around; in the awesome prairie thunderstorms, in the silent, eerie dance of the northern lights, the tabletop flat prairie of yellow grass and brightly painted elevators with grain trains rushing their loads to market. The winds blowing cold in winter, warm in spring, hot in summer, cooler in autumn were endless. Where did they come from? Where did they go? Who did they touch? Did they encircle the world? The swirling prairie winds encircled Scandinavia, Minnesota and Saskatchewan, bringing its squalling rains, winter blizzards, the sweet smell of clover hanging in the evening air and laundry blowing in the glowing sun.

Wheat field on the Saskatchewan prairie

My parent's (Lily and August) first home was a small house in the center of Yellow Grass. I don't remember the first home I lived in. I only remember what my mother told me. It was a small two room building where my Dad lived before he married my mother. She told of how she enjoyed hanging curtains and braiding rugs for the floor. She loved redecorating this home using her sewing, crocheting, and cooking talents. All signs of bachelorhood were gone. Dad had a dray business and did some carpenter work but wanted to try farming.

They enjoyed singing. She would tease him by singing *"I married you for your black mustache, you married me for gold. You married me for gold, you married me for gold, I married you for your black mustache you married me for gold."* Little did she know of the pioneer life she would be living on the prairies of Southern Saskatchewan or that she would not see her mother or family for fourteen years.

My Mother wrote often to her mother, Anna, and anxiously waited for her return letters. She told Anna about the snowstorms, the below zero weather and the wind. After she became pregnant she yearned for her mother and was lonesome. Anna was so pleased to hear that she would be a grandmother for the first time and wrote encouraging letters to Lily.

It took quite a while to find new friends. After her first visit to Dr. Allen they became friends. He and his wife were childless. He loved ministering to pregnant women and cheered Lily up with each visit.

On October 23, 1913 I, Hilda Amanda, was born at two o'clock in the morning. They named me after Dad's sister and mother. An announcement was sent to my grandmother, Anna. She was so thrilled and wanted a picture; which was readily taken and sent off. Grandma Anna kept me supplied with booties, shoes and dresses in every color of the rainbow. The pastel dresses were made from lawn or handkerchief linen. Some had lots of small tucks, others were hand embroidered and decorated with lace and ribbons. Some booties were crocheted, others knitted and some were made of felt and soft leather. My mother and father were most appreciative of these gifts, as living was sparse and not easy. Having a baby to care for helped Mom from being so lonesome.

Shortly after my first birthday, my Mom became pregnant again. On August 8, 1915 Daniel was born, on her birthday! Now she had two little ones to care for. She and Dad had become friends with a Danish family also named Hanson. Mrs. Hanson was in her late thirties and often helped Lily from being lonesome and tied down.

Small house in Yellow Grass

Some time after Daniel was born, Mom and Dad planned and decided to start wheat farming. Dr. Allen owned a three-quarter section of land and encouraged them to rent it, which they did. This land was located seventeen miles southwest of Yellow Grass near Cedoux. This was predominately a Polish Catholic community with a scattering of Irish and Swedes in the rural area.

It was a cold and windy day in March when they set out for their new home in the country. There had not been a previous visit to the farm. They knew there was a barn and a small house. We all rode on the wagon, which was heavily loaded. We were dressed warmly and snuggled up in blankets to keep warm on the open wagon. The ride seemed endless; 17 miles is a long way on poor roads. We arrived before dark.

The home we lived in was near Cedoux and the source of the Souris River on the Lamb farm. Dr. Allen had purchased the farm several years earlier from Mr. Lamb. The house was a granary type house with two rooms, no chimney, and no insulation. The stovepipe went through a fire proof sleeve-type apparatus that went through the roof. There was no chimney, so once in a while a fire started where the stovepipe went through the roof. There was also a barn on this property but no trees. The home was in poor condition. The bottom pane of the north window was out so a pillow and blanket were stuffed into that space to keep out the cold northern wind. Obviously, the first article unloaded was the stove. After the stove was set up a fire was started since it was very cold in the house.

Dad fed the horses, as he was to return to Yellow Grass after the wagon was unloaded. He worried about his family as he prepared to return to Yellow Grass for another load. "Are you sure you will be all right," he asked Lily. Lily cheered him on his way by singing, *I married you for your black mustache, and you married me for gold."* "We will be just fine," as she kissed him good-bye, "see you late tomorrow."

Before Dad left for another load, a fire was started in the cook stove to warm us up along with some warm food. The bed was put up with many quilts. It took quite a while for the house to get the least bit warm. We were still hungry so Mom cooked some rye meal mush to help warm us up. Then we dressed into warm flannel pajamas and crept into bed. My mother was a very loving mother. She slept in the middle of the bed with a child on each side of her. We loved to snuggle up to her so we could listen to her sing and tell bedtime stories; hugging, kissing and feeling her breasts comforted us—Daniel was still nursing.

We had not been in bed very long when the howling began. It was a terrifying eerie chorus of coyotes. "Will they come in through that stuffed window?" "No, no, no " she answered, "Listen and I'll tell you about coyotes, your Dad told me all about coyotes." "Coyotes are wild barking dogs. They can run real fast, faster than a wolf or fox. This cunning, strong leaper vocalizes from dusk to dawn with a distinctive series of barks, howls, and yelps that sometimes harmonizes. They stand two feet tall, live by pouncing and feeding on smaller animals, insects, fruit and carrion." "What is carrion?" I asked. "It is dead animals or birds", she said. She continued on describing coyotes. "They mate for life and have large families. They live in wide mouthed dens tunneled in riverbeds and gulches. If their area becomes disturbed they leave immediately and find another den. According to Indian folklore this crafty creature will be the last animal remaining on earth."

Daniel was asleep by now but I was still awake and thankful the window was stuffed shut. The endless night broke into morning; the sun shining always makes things look brighter. Mother was busy all day emptying boxes and putting things away. Furniture was meager; table and four chairs, high chair, another bed, a rocking chair, chaise lounge, treadle sewing machine, coal box, a work table and throw rugs my Mother had crocheted out of old clothing and blankets.

Orange crates and boxes served for cupboards and dressers. There was little clothing, only what was necessary, sewn by my mother out of discarded clothing from Dr. and Mrs. Allen. Food was mostly the basics, flour (white, wheat, and rye) sugar, lard, coffee, tea, molasses, syrup, oatmeal, prunes and raisins, some canned fish and meat. The second load Dad brought the next day was hay and grain for the horses, coal for the stove and canned food. For several days the children cried for milk, there was none.

We lived in this home until after Rudolph (Rudy) and Florence were born. Daniel and I were two years apart so the best that I can figure is we moved there in the early spring of 1916 and lived there until after Florence was born in 1925, so we probably lived there for ten or more years. Many improvements had been made during that time.

SWEDISH PANCAKES
3 eggs
1 cup flour
½ teaspoon salt
2 cups milk
6 tablespoons butter melted
Beat eggs and ½ cup milk with whisk. Add the flour and beat smooth. Beat in the rest of the ingredients. Heat pan (medium flame). Drop a ¼ cup of batter in a crepe pan and swirl around. When edges begin to brown, turn and cook another minute. Serve with lingonberries, strawberries, peaches or apple sauce. Top with whipped cream. Good with just syrup too.

My Dad applied and received a loan from the bank in Yellow Grass. He often thought about this land of opportunity and freedom of worship where in Sweden the wishes of the church and the laws of the Crown were one and the same. He was not the devout Christian that my Mother was, but was thankful for the freedom he had in this new land. His first purchase was a milk cow, which was a necessity. Plymouth Rock chickens were the next purchase. Now Mom was in business as far as cooking was concerned. By not living in town anymore with Cedoux four miles away, food lists were necessary.

My Dad started going to auction sales shopping for horses and machinery, all necessary for his new venture in farming. Most of the horses were Broncos that had to be broken to harness. It took lots of patience and a quiet team to put up with a wild stubborn Bronco. He needed a minimum of twelve horses. Mares were definitely a wise purchase as they could be bred to increase the herd. He purchased geldings only if they would match up with a mare in color, breed and markings. The mares were bred every spring by a traveling stallion. The stallion was tied to a horse drawn buggy, driven by a man who owned it. They stayed for a few days until the mares were bred. We children were not allowed to watch any

35

of that business. Dad just pointed his hand to the house; we knew that meant to stay out of sight—although curiosity almost killed us.

Spring came or at least the snow was gone nearly overnight. The warm Chinook winds melted inches of snow overnight, leaving water everywhere. Chinook winds are a warm dry wind that descends the eastern slopes of the Rocky Mountains. It is just amazing how fast the deep snow would melt, leaving tracks as the "crow flies" roads were made over winter. In the wintertime when the ground is covered with lots of snow, everywhere they traveled was "as the crow flies". The roads were never plowed. The fields were unfenced, so the horses' noses were pointed in the direction they were going. Doing this cut off several miles no matter where or what direction they went. Roads were straight and followed section and correction lines. The compacted snow resembled railroad tracks. It took longer for those tracks to melt, as they were ice-packed.

It was shortly after this melted my parents realized their home was situated at the source of the Souris River. This small river was a source of much enjoyment for us—playing in the water and catching frogs. The land Dad rented was flat and fertile. One could see for miles and miles on this treeless plain. The prairie was rich in buffalo grass and some cactus. Their waxy yellow blossoms were so beautiful in spring along with popular lavender and white crocus.

The greatest resource of this farm was the well. It was dug deeply. It also served as a refrigerator as ice remained in this well all summer. Perishable food was placed in a pail and lowered down on the ice by a rope. Water for the house and animals was gathered from the well, by a pail. This took a lot of practice to be able to drop the pail just right so that it would fill and then pull it up by rope. The animals drank from a trough when the water was low or dry in what we called the creek, which was really the source of Souris River.

Late in the summer my Mom and Dad began talking and preparing for a baby that was expected sometime in November. The sun shone brightly on the brisk cold day of November 16, 1917. Mom was as busy as a bee. She washed the clothing, cleaned and baked many loaves of bread. Towards evening she was definite the baby would be born the next day. Daniel and I were under her feet all day and getting into trouble. It was too cold to put us out to play. November was usually a cold, windy, and snowy month. We plagued her all day with questions because things were somewhat unusual. Monday was always laundry day, Saturday was baking day, but these tasks were being done on a different day than normal.

Later in the evening Mom told Dad she was experiencing the first signs of delivery. "We will leave early in the morning", she said, "because I would really dread bundling up the children in the middle of the night." November 17— The day was cold and sunny. Bricks were put in the oven. Mom packed and Dad harnessed the team. They would be staying overnight or until the baby was born. The warm bricks were wrapped in paper and placed on the floor of the sleigh to keep our feet warm. Buffalo robes were great to be wrapped up in as they kept out the wind. They were also very heavy. Arriving in the late afternoon, Mom, Daniel, and I were left at the nurse's home next door to Dr. Allen's home. Dad left the horses at the livery stable where they were watered and fed.

Dad, Daniel, and I had supper with the Doctor and Mrs. Allen; the three of us were to stay at the nurses home and were all to sleep in a downstairs hall room where we could see into the bedroom where Mom was in bed. About eight o'clock Dr. Allen arrived carrying a black satchel. "What has he got in that black bag?" I asked Dad. He answered "he has Rudy in that bag." Then the door was closed to my mother's bedroom so we could not see what was happening. Somewhat later they heard a baby cry and Dr. Allen said, "It's a boy." I never could figure out how my Dad knew Rudy was in the black bag. I was only four years old but never forgot it. Two weeks later Dad bundled Daniel and I up to go after my Mom and bring her and the baby home.

GRAT
1 quart of whole milk
Salt to taste
Flour to make a thick sauce

Dan, Rudy and I ate a lot of this as kids. Put the Grat on a plate with a large pat of butter in the middle with a spoon go around the edge and dip in the melted butter. Florence and I still have this at least once a year.

In the early 1920s my mother became very sick. At first Dr. Allen was not called. However, when she broke out with boil-like sores all over her body, both she and my dad became very frightened. After Dr. Allen did a variety of tests, right there at the home with us and Dad watching his every move. My mother's condition was diagnosed as Black Small Pox.

"Everyone will have to be vaccinated and a quarantine sign put up on the outside door to warn others there is a transmittable disease in this house," the doctor stated. Of course we were all frightened and cried as we were stabbed with the vaccination needle. My mother was very sick and could easily have died. We did not attend school until the quarantine was lifted. No one was allowed to enter our home during this time. Dr. Allen came many times to check on us and to leave food and medicine. I was the only one who got a couple of pox on my forehead. What a relief it was for everyone when my mother's sores were gone and the sign on the door was removed.

"Now", Dr. Allen explained, "you must spend a long day out of this house. Is there a neighbor that you can go to for a whole day while I fumigate this house?" Dr. Allen planned on applying a smoke to destroy the germs and disinfect the house. Dad consulted the Bloodgoods who lived north and across the railroad tracks from us. They agreed to take us in for the day. The Bloodgoods had children too so this was an exciting day for all, especially having been confined to our home for over a month. We returned home after dusk. There was a strange odor remaining in the house so the doors and windows were opened to air it out. We still experienced some burning in our eyes. Dr. Allen used a very toxic gas that had an offensive and intense odor.

The family rejoiced and laughed when they went to bed thanking God for Dr. Allen and the loving care he had given us, especially for saving our mother from this deadly disease. Even though it took her a while to get her strength back, it was the end of Black Small Pox with very little scarring.

Harvesting wheat
with a horsedrawn binder

On Christmas Eve day we had a big chore to do. Hay had to be scattered in the yard near the house on top of the snow for the reindeer to eat while Santa was in the house delivering presents. Mom was busy preparing the yearly gourmet supper. This consisted of Swedish meatballs, potatoes and gravy, rice and suet puddings, special Christmas bread, apples and Japanese oranges. Quite a treat from usual rye meal mush.

Santa was a tall, slim man wrapped in a red blanket. He had a beard and a stocking cap on his head. We each received a new toothbrush, toothpaste, a pencil and candy. He always kissed us good-bye and in the morning all the hay was gone with sleigh and hoof marks all over. I finally realized Santa was my dad because of the tobacco taste of his kiss.

He must have got up after we were asleep and took care of the evidence, then lead the cow around to make all those hoof marks. I never told my brothers about Dad being Santa Claus. Santa always had to enter by the door because there was not a chimney in this house. Christmas vacation was spent playing checkers and cutting out paper snowflakes and the like. The most popular outdoor game was "Fox and the Goose", when the weather was bearable, otherwise we played in the barn where Dad had put up a swing. Many times we fed the horses and carried in large chunks of snow. The horses chewed the snow, as there was no water. All the water used for the household and the cow was melted snow.

BAKED RICE PUDDING

3 eggs
2 cups milk
1 cup cooked rice
¼ teaspoon salt
1 teaspoon vanilla
½ cup raisins

Beat eggs. Combine other ingredients. Pour into buttered baking dish. Sprinkle with cinnamon and bake at 325 degrees for 30 to 40 minutes.

EBLESKIVER

1 package yeast in ¼ cup warm water
3 cups whole milk
1 cup of half and half
¼ cup sugar
1 scant teaspoon salt
2 cups raisins soaked in hot water
6 eggs separated
½ teaspoon cardamom

4 cups flour—fold in beaten egg whites in last
Drop dough in cups of Ebelskiver pan

FATTIGMAN
1 whole egg
4 egg yolks
4 teaspoons of sugar
4 tablespoons of cream
1 ¾ cup flour
1 teaspoon almond flavoring
½ teaspoon salt
Divide in half and roll out to 1/8 inch thickness. Cut strips with a slit in the middle. Fry in hot oil. Drain. Sprinkle with powdered sugar.

In 1924 I was in the fifth grade and Daniel and Rudy were in school too. We had several ways of getting to school. The most likely ways were horses hitched in a team, horseback, and walking. Every school had a barn where the horses were housed and fed while the children were in school from nine in the morning until four in the afternoon. School started in the middle of August and continued until the end of June.

When fall work was done at freeze up we were allowed to drive horses to school. All the horses were young. Counting colts, yearlings and workhorses our family owned thirty or more horses. The horses were assembled in a team of two or more to pull a wagon, buggy, sleigh, or stoneboat. The only problem was a "run-a-way", which are very frightening experiences to live through. Something would frighten the team such as a rabbit or a barking dog and they would run and kick as fast as they could. Most grown men cannot control a run-a-way horse. The first "run-a-way" pretty much finished the buggy. By spring we were down to a stoneboat—a low platform contraption on skids with no tongue. This contraption was used mostly for hauling barrels of water or picking rocks. When the snow was slippery we could not use it since it would slide into the hind legs of the horses, which was dangerous.

Another option was riding horseback. The lunch boxes, really empty jam cans, were snapped on to the horses halter as they also carried oats for the horses. My Dad bragged about my horsemanship. I loved horses.

When the horses were used for fieldwork, haying and harvesting, we walked to school. Shoes were not used when school was out because they were saved for school. Going barefoot all summer really toughened the soles of our feet. We shocked wheat barefooted and our legs got all scratched up from the stubble and thistles. Many times when school started our feet had grown out of our shoes; so we went barefoot until it got cold. Sometimes we wore two pair of long black stockings, the second pair rolled down to the ankle. Most of our shoes were bought through a catalog after Dad received a check for the wheat that had been harvested in the fall.

Connor School House

Mother made most of our clothing. Flannel and long legged fleece lined underwear and long black stockings and shoes were ordered from either the Simpson and Co, Ltd. or Eatons. Mom made all of our outerwear too. She used a razor blade to cut the threads in the seams of used clothing while I helped hold the seams tight. It did not take very long to rip a large coat apart. She was a genius when it came to sewing. She never used a purchased pattern. She made her own patterns out of paper. She cut the material so that the inside of the used clothing was outside which did not show wear. All the coats, boys' pants and shirts were made out of used clothing.

My winter dresses were made from purchased navy wool serge. Two bib aprons made from used sturdy cotton completed my winter wear. I detested the long legged underwear; by the end of the week one could wrap the legs nearly twice around the ankle making my legs lumpy. That did not bother the boys—they wore pants so the lumps were hidden. Most of the used coats, dresses, and other material came from Doctor and Mrs. Allen. My summer dresses were made from Mrs. Allen's (what she called worn out) dresses.

Mother was a hard worker raising her family without many conveniences. She remained a very attractive lady and was held in high esteem. When short hair became popular Dad gave her a blunt short hair cut, which was not too complimentary. He could do many things well, but cutting hair was not his forte. Her dresses were made with a dropped waistline with box pleats on the side. She wore a hat whenever they went to church, which was not in the wintertime.

HOT MILK CAKE
1 cup milk
1/8 pound butter
2 cups sugar
4 eggs
2 teaspoons baking powder
2 cups flour
1 teaspoon vanilla

ICING FOR HOT MILK CAKE
1 8 ounce package cream cheese
½ cup margarine
1 cup confectioners sugar
Heat milk and butter in a saucepan until butter melts. Beat sugar and eggs until creamy. Add Baking powder and flour to sugar and egg mixture, then add milk and butter. Mix—add vanilla. Bake in a tube pan at 325 to 350 degrees for 30 minutes. Do not peek into oven during this period. Bake 15 to 20 minutes longer. Test for doneness.

While we lived here we met and enjoyed picnics with Swedish friends. Dad played an accordion and Erick Wickstrom played the fiddle. When the granaries were empty we learned to dance. This included the waltz, polka, and fox trot.

I received my elementary education at Cedoux School and Connor School. These schools were in a predominately Polish and Catholic community. The Connor School was also built while we lived here. This meant we had a shorter distance to school. Then a bridge was built over the Souris River, which we had to cross to get to school, so no more standing on the buggy seat to avoid getting wet when the water was high.

School days opened with the singing of "Oh Canada", and "God Save the King and Queen." The school district or government furnished pencils and paper. Paper was never wasted. Most of the schoolwork was done at the blackboard or slate before written on paper, which generally were tests. Beads were also used.

Discipline was very strict. I was never a victim of the hame strap, but my brother Rudy was often told to walk up to the front and receive an allotted number of lashes on each open hand. My heart went out to him. He was a small tow-headed boy and walked up like a man, took his lashes and embarrassment before all. Swearing or dirty language of any kind was not accepted. Rudy would swear out loud whenever he made a mistake in his schoolwork—he just could not refrain whether he swore in English or Polish. We learned many Polish words—some were carved on the desktops.

We were the only Protestants at the school we attended. The rest were Catholic, mostly Polish. Once I caught the Catholic boys taking our Protestantism out on our horses as they were tied in the school barn, by hitting them with sticks and straps. I told the teacher which brought an end to that kind of treatment.

One evening after school they threatened us saying, "If you come to school tomorrow you'll be very sorry." We were frightened and told Dad about it, stating we probably should stay home a day. We got no sympathy from him. "You three kids just go to school and show them how fearless you Swedes are." The next morning we started to school on foot as it was planting time and the horses were used for that. As we approached the school we could see two lines of children lined up on both sides of the path. Rudy asked, "What shall we do?" I said, "We will just walk like always. Rudy go first, Dan second and I'll bring up the rear." So we did—no one touched us. I think they were surprised or just testing us. No religious based pranks were pulled on us anymore. We were accepted!

In school we took many subjects. Graduation from eighth grade required passing a test in thirteen subjects. History books consisted of Ancient, Modern, English, American and Canadian. I enjoyed drawing maps of countries in geography especially Canada and the United States and the whole American continent. Each day went on as usual except when the school inspector arrived unannounced. He would arrive early to listen to opening exercises and then took over as teacher of the day. He gave an exam for each class first through eighth grade and corrected them. He had the power or authority to promote or demote any student, which he often did. The pupils were the most quiet and well behaved on this day compared to any other day in the whole year. All of us lived in awe of this man, including the teacher, who was reprimanded if the teaching did not meet his standards.

During recess we played games, which included skipping, single or double and triple with one person turning the rope. Other times two persons would twirl the rope and the rest would run in, jump, and run out, trying not to trip. This would keep on until all but one was eliminated and announced a winner. Softball was also played. Connor school kids played against Cedoux kids. When we played ball we had yells. The Connor School yell was "One, Two, Three, Four, Five, Six, Seven, all good children go to heaven. When they get there they will say Connor school kids sure can play. Rah! Rah! Rah!"

Other games played in summer were "Last Couple Out",

"Drop the Handkerchief," "Three Deep", "Anti I Over", "Kick the Can"; to name a few. In the winter we played "Fox and Goose", had snowball fights, built forts and igloos and rode down straw stacks on sleds. No one ever drove them anywhere. We walked to and from school then home to do chores. Our parents strongly believed in "spare the rod and spoil the child", "early to bed and early to rise makes a man healthy, wealthy, and wise," "waste not, want not," and "go to the ant thou sluggard, consider her ways and be wise" Proverbs 6:6.

At home I would wrestle with my brothers. I could hold both of them down, even after we were eight, ten and twelve years of age. I was the oldest, Rudy the youngest. My brother Dan was roly-poly and Rudy was short and thin. Dan had a mop of curly hair, which he disliked, Rudy and I had thick wavy hair.

The three of us enjoyed playing in the water of the Souris, catching frogs and toads and sometimes riding a pig into the water. We didn't have many toys to play with so a lot of our time was spent in coloring books and drawing. We always had a dog and kittens to play with, and horses to feed, curry and ride.

In the winter we played in the barn. It was in this barn that I learned how to curry and care for horses, including harnessing. It was also in this barn that Dad broke his arm by a horse pushing him against a wall. We played "ball" in the barn, the difference being instead of batting a ball we batted "horse apples" (frozen horse manure) out the barn door. Four horses were stabled in the winter. The other twenty-four head or more ran free on the open range all winter finding shelter around straw stacks. There was a horse roundup in the spring. Quite often Dad could tell someone had used some of the horses during the winter by the harness and collar marks and manure stains. Sometimes children played with the calves hanging onto their tails and running around in the barn to keep warm.

One time when I was running behind a calf hanging onto its tail, it ran under a harness pole and the steel chain at the end of the tug hit me in the mouth. I stopped to spit out pieces of tooth, and there was pain. I was so frightened and didn't know what to do as my lip was bleeding too. I left the barn and went to the house. Trying to hide this disaster from Dad was fruitless because the pain in that tooth was unbearable. The tongue-lashing I received from him did not help matters either. My dear mother gave me love and understanding. That was a comfort. The dentist said it was a bad break and decided to kill the nerve and take away the pain. Over half of the tooth right in front was gone. After several trips to the dentist I ended up with half a gold tooth. I did not like the trips to the dentist in Weyburn; they were painful and I hated that half-gold tooth too.

Next to horseback riding I loved to run, especially after a rainfall when I went barefoot. I ran a lot in Saskatchewan. In the wintertime I ran following jackrabbit tracks. Even if I saw one I never caught one. I was quite wiry and very thin, being five foot two and one hundred pounds, I could really run fast. I was nicknamed "killdeer" after the bird because I had skinny legs and always ran.

Dan, Lily, Hilda, Rudy, August

Right after New Years my Mother and Father started making plans for her birthing of their fourth child in January 1925. Noticing my mother getting more tired and changing her shape in the late autumn I got curious. Now at age twelve, when Daniel and Rudy were born I was ignorant or too young to realize. I began to ask questions and did get some answers; at least enough to know where babies come from other than black bags. When I was soon to be a teenager, my mother approached me one morning and said "Hilda, I would like you to read some of these chapters in this doctor book." The chapters I was to read were on menstruation, pregnancy and female diseases. As I read about this bleeding every month I cried "Why me?" "I don't want this. I wish I was a boy."

My mother was expecting in January 1925. She knitted, crocheted and sewed clothing for the expected one. Much depended on the weather so when the winds died down and the snow was not drifting they decided this was the time to go. As usual hot bricks were put into the oven to keep our feet warm. Soon we were on our merry way to Yellow Grass.

This time we were all to stay at Dr. Allen's home. Doctor and Mrs. Allen were wonderful. He was a jolly, beardless Santa Claus type fellow. His face was ruddy and had some wrinkles around his eyes. We all loved him. His wife was slim and trim. She was nearly as tall as he was; he looked short alongside Dad though. They had a beautiful home with lovely furniture. The Allen's were childless so we were made to understand there would be no rough housing; respect for other people's property was drilled into our heads. We were to display good manners.

I never forgot that first breakfast. Doctor Allen sat at the head of the table and said grace. His wife dished up oatmeal and placed a dish in front of each of us including the Doctor. "Where is my bowl?" he jostled. "Please give me my bowl, I cannot eat oatmeal out of this bowl." She got him his everyday bowl, and then he was content. He turned his bowl as he ate and somehow this old bowl just fit his hand.

One time when we were visiting them, Dr. Allen was anxious to show us the male kitten someone had given him, named Barney. It slept in his car in the garage. Some months later he had a big surprise. Once when he got in his car, there on the front seat of his car was his "male" cat with a bunch of kittens. Every Friday he would go up to town and buy fish for Barney. Can you imagine the kidding he received from the grocer? It was all over town that Dr. Allen's "male" cat had a batch of kittens. We also had dinner at their home, after attending church that was located back of the park across from Dr. Allen's home. This park was later named after him.

Dr. Allen Park

My mother stayed at the nurse's home while waiting for the baby to be born. We returned home with Dad. It took a long time for that baby to be born, but she finally arrived on January 25, 1925.

It was interesting to learn how Mom and Dad named their children. They would each place a name in a hat—first for a boy and then for a girl, then they drew out a name for each sex. Dad won out with the first three, Swedish names of course, Hilda, Daniel and Rudolph. This time Mom drew her name—Florence May. We could hardly wait until we saw our sister. I thought she had the most beautiful name. She was named after Dr. Allen's niece, Florence May, who was my sixth grade teacher.

When Florence was a couple days old, and the weather was milder, we bundled up and went to Yellow Grass to visit our mother and see the new baby at the nurse's home. I got to hold her. She was the most beautiful doll I had ever seen with big blue eyes. We stayed overnight and went back the next day—without Mom and the baby.

We missed Mom so much—we were all really 'Mom-sick'. The worst part was the food. One morning for example, the milk was sour. Dad heated it up—like magic we had curds and whey; we did eat it when a little syrup was added. Most of the school lunches were unequaled; for example sliced raw prunes or apples on bread and pickled eggs. By the time we reached the school three to five miles away, the lunches were frozen. Lunch buckets lined the floor near the heat register, which took until noon to thaw out. Action games were played in the mornings to keep warm.

It had been an unusually cold and windy winter, which probably meant that venturing out on a long journey to Yellow Grass was out. The day Dad went to bring Mom and Florence home was balmy. Chinook winds blew during the night and melted most of the snow.

Mrs. Bloodgood came over that day and we washed everything in the house. She brought over the biggest piece of meat I had ever seen. It was a fresh whole ham with the rind left on. It baked slowly in the oven most of the day while we washed and hung out the wash wading in ankle deep water. It was just amazing how fast the deep snow would melt. Everytime I entered the house the pleasant aroma of baking roast permeated the house, making my mouth water.

All was in order, clothes folded, ironed and put away. Supper was ready when they arrived home. How happy we all were to see Mom—like someone back from the dead. It was an especially happy time as we all sat around the table enjoying that supper and homecoming. The roast was perfect; the rind was crisp and delicious. The rich brown gravy over mashed potatoes was delectable. It was the end of Dad's cooking.

Florence slept with Mom and Dad. Mom nursed all of her babies. It was not too long before Florence and I slept together on the new chaise lounge in the kitchen. She was my live doll. I could rock her, change her, and play with her. When she cried before nursing times, I could hold her and give her a sugar lump wrapped in cloth and rock her to sleep. In the summer of 1925, I rode horseback, Florence in my arms. I was thrilled when she started to talk and called me Manda.

Hilda and Florence on horseback

Spring on the Saskatchewan prairie is beautiful and exciting. Crocuses, swaying in the breeze, resembled waves on the gray blue lake. Birds singing, especially the meadowlarks, and building nests. And gophers were out of hibernation.

My brothers and I spent many a spring morning on a gopher hunt. It did not take long to harness Fred and Nigger, and to fill the large fifty gallon wooden barrel with water. I was the teamster. The team was hitched to the stoneboat with the water barrel loaded on it and a couple of pails. I loved horses and the out of doors; but hated killing gophers and pulling off their tails. Blackie, our one eyed dog, ran in front of the horses barking and wagging his tail. His job was to chase the gophers into a hole. Its life was spared for a few minutes.

I would drive the team near the hole. The boys filled the gallon pails from the barrel and poured the water into the gopher hole. Blackie stood very close with his head cocked waiting for the gopher to come gasping out of his hole. Blackie got him as soon as his head appeared. Rudy pulled off his tail and stuck it into a paper bag.

We would then get back on the stoneboat and ride around for a few minutes until we found another heavily populated gopher area. Daniel and Rudy plugged some of the holes with dirt thus minimizing the number of holes for the gophers to come out of. Blackie stood real close to a hole poised for action. I poured water into several holes— in no time gophers came out sneezing, snorting and gasping out of the half dozen holes. Blackie bounded and scampered between several holes. He was barking and snapping his teeth like mad. Daniel and Rudy were swinging clubs, hitting some and missing others. I jumped up and down laughing and watching the excitement. The two old horses stood dozing with droping heads. Dead gophers were strewn on the ground. When the excitement subsided, the tail count was over a dozen. We used good judgment in using the old team because young horses would no doubt have run away with all that noise.

We generally spent a whole day hunting gophers. At noontime we sat on the ground to rest and eat our prune sandwiches. We bragged about what a smart dog Blackie was and talked about the time he lost his eye after being kicked by a horse. We even shared our sandwiches with him—he was panting and drank lots of water. Blackie loved to be petted. How we loved that small longhaired dog.

When the sun started to go down we headed the team for home. We were all tired and glad to ride, Blackie included. The gophers we hunted were quite large and not striped. They were called "flicker tails". The Province paid a bounty for the tails, some years as much as a nickel a tail. Rat-tails were a quarter; unfortunately we never caught any. Gophers did damage to crops, they ate the tender green plants of wheat, oats or barley. Often times horses would accidentally step in a gopher hole and break a leg or receive a bad sprain.

Dad kept Fred, a white gelding, and Nigger a black gelding with a white star on his forehead, especially for us to drive. Otherwise nearly all the horses were young and frisky. This particular day 130 gophers were killed earning us three dollars and twenty-five cents. Enough to buy each of us a new pair of shoes. Later that day I rode horseback into Cedoux with the gopher tails and picked up the mail, which we received once a week.

We all agreed that gopher hunting was profitable. Regardless of the hard work, it was fun and we each did our part. I never killed a gopher or pulled off tails—choosing to take care of the horses instead, currying, harnessing and feeding them. That was my joy.

Besides killing gophers, another method of raising money was killing potato bugs. A big garden was a necessity because vegetables and potatoes were stored, canned or dried to last a year. Mom also insisted on planting citron. She made a tasty sauce out of this fruit. When we planted potatoes Dad used a one fallow plow pulled buy a team and we children dropped potato seeds into the shallow furrow. Then when the second row was made the plow covered the first furrow. The worst part of the garden was the weeding and killing potato bugs.

Before the blooming stage, my dad watched the potato plants with an eagle eye. The first bugs what came were large beetle-type with a hard shell. They laid light yellow colored eggs under the leaves. The hatchlings were dark red, rubbery, ugly things. The longer they lived the bigger they got. Sometimes nearly all the leaves would be stripped off plants. The method we used was this: each of us was armed with a can with an inch of kerosene in it and a wooden shingle. We would walk up and down the rows, slap the leaves with the shingle and the bugs would fall into the kerosene.

Dad paid us according to the number of bugs each had. I always won everything my dad challenged me to do. Daniel was one and three quarter years younger than me, but two years older than Rudy. Daniel was always last. When we had gone over the patch more than once to be sure all bugs were gone—Dad would put a lighted match into each can and burn up the bugs. Turning over the leaves and smashing the eggs was gruesome.

We also got paid to weed the garden. We did not chop the weeds off with a hoe. Dad taught us the best way to kill weeds was to pull them up, roots and all. We crawled on our knees and pulled the weeds up by the roots layering them, exposing the roots to the sun so the danger of their taking root was abolished. We generally did this after a rain, as the weeds pulled easier. Pulling weeds was also another way of having spending money for the Weyburn fair. The biggest treat we ever had was sweet corn dipped in melted butter, Umm-yum! We were never paid for anything else nor did we get an allowance. Responsibility was taught early. We never quibbled about who cleaned the barn and pumped or hauled water.

CREAM OF POTATO SOUP
5 large potatoes
½ cup sliced carrots
6 slices of bacon
1 cup of chopped onions
1 cup sliced celery
1 ½ teaspoon salt
¼ teaspoon pepper
2 cups milk
2 cups light cream or evaporated milk
Cheddar cheese (shredded)
Parsley

Wash, pare and slice potatoes. Cook with carrots in boiling water and cover until tender. Sauté bacon until crisp, drain on paper and crumble. Combine all ingredients except cheese and parsley. Simmer 30 minutes. Garnish each serving with cheese and parsley.

During the spring and summer months Mom and I did missionary work. Mom organized the study group because she thought it was necessary to teach Bible to the Protestant ladies. She was the Bible teacher and I was the song leader. The Catholic Church was north of Cedoux and Protestant churches were located in Weyburn and Yellow Grass—too distant to attend regularly. This group consisted of a dozen or so Swedish ladies. They each took their turn entertaining in their homes.

Besides teaching the ladies new songs, I had to sing a solo with no musical accompaniment. Sometimes, but not often, I would start in too high a key, so the veins would stick out on my throat, which made me feel embarrassed. They always requested that I sing *Bringing in the Sheaves*. The words were: *Sowing in the morning, sowing seeds of kindness, sowing in the noon-tide and the dewy eve. Waiting for the harvest, and the time of reaping, we shall come rejoicing, bringing in the sheaves.* Chorus: *Bringing in the sheaves, bringing in the sheaves, we shall come rejoicing, bringing in the sheaves.* It could be they associated this song with wheat sheaves, as they were all wheat farmers. Saskatchewan is still noted for its wheat.

After Bible study and sing time the hostess served a delicious lunch. We got to each destination by horse and buggy. Mother drove a mare named Jip. She was a pacer and a very good buggy horse, but had to be held as she was anxious to go. When she got her hitched to the buggy, Dad had to hold her until we got in the seat because she took off like a flash and kept up that pace until they arrived at their destination. Then one of the men would hold her in the same way when they went home.

One part of the road followed the railroad tracks between Cedoux and Colfax for about a mile. Mother just hoped and prayed that a train would not come because Jip did not like trains. She would inevitably kick out the dashboard and take off at top speed for home. It really was not a run-a-away but had she swerved one way or another they could have tipped over and probably been hurt. On one occasion Mom's foot got caught in the front wheel as Jip started off as Dad did not have a strong hold on her bridle. Her foot went partly around the wheel resulting in a badly broken ankle. Dr. Allen set it well. It took a long time to heal, but evidently he did a good job since she never limped or had a crooked foot. Even when her foot was in a cast we kept up our missionary work each week.

We went to church in the summer time to Yellow Grass, which always turned out to be a festive time with Dr. Allen and his wife. The children played in the park across from their house. My Mother was a strong religious believer whereas Dad was the opposite. She got nowhere with him but she taught us to thank God for food and to say our prayers at night.

ANGEL FOOD PIE
4 ½ tablespoons corn starch
¾ cups sugar
1 ½ cups hot water
3 egg whites
3 teaspoons sugar
Pinch of salt
1 teaspoon vanilla
Put corn starch, sugar and hot water in top of double boiler and cook until thick and clear. Beat egg whites until light, add salt, sugar and vanilla and beat until creamy. Add hot mixture slowly to egg whites, beating continuously. Cool slightly and pour into baked pie shell. Put whipped cream and nuts on top.

Much like when the school inspector arrived, another dreaded day at school was when the Red Cross nurse visited each year in the spring. Each student was given hearing, eye, and throat tests. Rudy and I were unfortunate to have both tonsils and adenoids. We were thankful that our hearing and sight passed inspection. Daniel's health was perfect. The Red Cross set up a day early in July for a mass operation day to remove tonsils and adenoids. This way, hopefully, students would be all healed up by mid-August when school started.

When the dreaded day of tonsil and adenoid removal arrived all the children were assembled at the Cedoux Community Hall at nine o'clock. There were over twenty children registered. Twenty numbers were put into a hat where each child drew out a number. Rudy drew out number one and I drew number five. What a lottery!

The doctors and nurses were dressed in white. Cots were set up in rows all over the room with a white sheet and pillow on each cot. One of the office rooms served as the operating room. The majority of the children were frightened to death, some were crying and others clinging to their mother's skirts. When all was in order number one was announced and Rudy walked right in "the room". After the operation, I saw him being rolled out and placed on one of the cots. He was out cold and white as a ghost. Mom sat on a chair beside him. When number four was called Rudy started to wake up and vomited into the dish that my Mom held. It was a bloody mess. Mom and a nurse tried to calm him as he was crying.

That was "IT" for me. I was out the door like a bolt of lightening and started running for home as fast as I could go. Dad and a bachelor neighbor got into a Chevrolet car and started after me. They later told me that it was over two miles before they caught me. They called me killdeer for reason. Dad had to hang onto me as I continued to struggle to get away. It took four people to get me into that operating room. I didn't weigh more than eighty pounds, but I was very wiry and strong.

My heart was pounding so fast when I entered that room. They put me on the cot, placed an ether cone over my mouth and nose and I was told to start counting. When I got to one hundred I was told to start over again and heard someone say, "Boy oh boy, she is a tough one." Needless to say I lived through it and had a very sore throat for weeks. Jello was about the only food I could swallow besides water and milk.

I was skinny as a rail and after that surgery I became anemic. For many days after this event I had nightmares seeing a room full of kids, crying and vomiting blood—the "massacre" was over. This remained as one of the most terrifying days of my whole life. But it didn't affect my singing so I kept on accompanying Mother in our volunteer missionary work.

APPLESAUCE CAKE
2 cups flour
1 teaspoon cinnamon

c

¼ teaspoon cloves
½ teaspoon nutmeg
½ teaspoon salt
½ cup butter or shortening
1 cup sugar
1 egg
1 teaspoon baking soda
1 ½ cup applesauce
1 cup raisins
1 cup nut meats

Measure flour, add spices and salt, and sift together. Cream shortening and sugar. Beat in egg. Mix soda and applesauce–add creamed mixture alternating with flour. Add raisins and nuts. Bake in moderate oven 45 minutes.

Harvest time was a busy time for all the family. We learned to shock wheat at an early age. Dad hired shockers, which did not exempt us kids from doing our share. Dad also fired a lot of men. Each man had to be able to shock several acres a day or else someone else was hired. These men consisted of "Greenhorns" as they were called. They were emigrants from Europe consisting of Swedes, Poles, and Englishmen. Englishmen were hired last as August considered them lazy and many in fact were.

The horse-drawn grain binders cut and tied the wheat into bundles. These bundles were placed with the straw end down starting out with two placing them so they stood up. Then several, six or eight, bundles were placed around the two making a shock. One was considered a poor shocker if they fell down. When thrashing started the shocks were pitched into horse drawn hayracks and pulled up to the separator.

Those were steam engine days—these machines were huge. The wheels left tracks at least three feet or more wide. Dad worked as the separator man for the season. Then there was a waterman and a straw man that came with the thrashing rig. Getting all the belts in place, greasing all the wheels, gears, e.g. it was a big job for Dad; he was a super separator man. The waterman hauled water from the sloughs to keep the steam engine from getting thirsty. The straw man hauled the straw to the engine and pitched it into the volumous stomach. It took two tons of straw and gallons and gallons of water to keep this beast steaming.

This engine had a large flywheel where a wide belt was placed and then on a wheel on the separator. It took great talent to line up the engine and separator so the belt would stay on with the right amount of tightness. This belt got all the other belts on the separator in motion. It was a beautiful sight to watch the straw coming out of the blower on one end and wheat coming out of the pipe and emptying into a hundred-bushel wagon. Of course the wind played an important part too, blowing away from the action so that chaff and dust blew away from the men. Granaries were placed in the fields. The wheat went into them. My job was to haul the filled wagons to the elevators in Cedoux. I also had to water, feed, curry and harness my team.

Many times threshing went on late into the night. The straw stacks were set on fire making it possible for the men to see putting bundles into the separator. Threshing was also done early in the morning. When the raining season set in, all the men would go duck hunting. They cleaned the ducks and Mom prepared them. These men, eighteen or more slept in the bunkhouse that came along with the steam engine. Later on a cookhouse was added so Mom was relieved of that job.

We never ate with the threshers. We had our usual bread and milk. We also took turns milking the two cows and brought the milk into the house. A slice of homemade bread was placed on a plate, sugar spread over the bread and then warm unpasteurized milk. We never complained as this was taken for granted. Most of the time we were in bed and asleep when the men ate a full course meal including pie. Mom made several pies each morning. Lunch was served in the afternoon, usually consisting of sandwiches, pickles, cookies or cake and coffee. We children partook of this, since we brought it out to the field. When the pickles were beets, one of the men, an Englishman would drink the pickle juice when the jar was empty.

HARVARD BEETS
4 cups beet juice
2 cups of vinegar
4 cups sugar
Salt to taste
Combine ingredients and add sliced cooked beets. Bring to a good boil. Put in sterilized jars and seal.

REFRIGERATOR PICKLES
7 cups thinly sliced cukes
1 cup onions sliced
1 green pepper (optional)
1 tablespoon salt
Let stand for one hour
2 cups sugar
1 cup vinegar
1 tablespoon celery seed
Drain cukes and add vinegar sauce and refrigerate. It lasts a long time.

BOILED SALAD DRESSING
2 eggs
2 tablespoons flour
1 teaspoon salt
2 tablespoons butter
2/3 cup vinegar
1/3 cup water
½ cup sugar
1 teaspoon mustard

Mix the dry ingredients; add butter and beaten eggs and liquid. Cook in double boiler until thick. Thin with cream.

Many times while the men were sitting around on the ground eating and talking, I would have a live mouse by the tail and hold it down their back where it would scratch away trying to get away. By the time a man would get off the ground I was long gone—no one ever caught me.

I hauled many loads to the elevator. It was especially nice when the wheat was threshed into the wagon. I became very tired when I scooped that hundred-bushel wagon full out of the granary. Many times it was dark when I returned home—a line up at the elevator caused this. Mom was so happy when she could hear the wagon returning and the clip clop of the horses' feet. The closer to home we got, the faster the team went. When the horses were watered and fed I could go in and have my supper of bread and milk.

Depending on the weather, threshing generally lasted a couple of weeks. Sometimes a rainstorm would come up and strong wind would blow the shocks over. Hauling wheat continued long after the threshing was done. Some grain was stored for spring planting, and the animals, also for flour and cereal. Dad also harvested oats, barley, and flax.

During haying and threshing time some chaff or other foreign object would get into our eyes. Mom would place a flaxseed in our eye. When this happened to us we would lie down and go to sleep. When we woke up the flax and any foreign object was on the pillow. One year I had many very painful and ugly boils on my forearms. Mom would make a hot bread poultice and place on the boils. This took away most of the pain and cured them. When an infection was small Mom would split a raisin and put on the sore, which also drew out the pus.

c

HAM AND BEAN VEGETABLE SOUP
1 pound navy beans (2 ½ cups)
8 cups water
1 ½ pounds meaty smoked pork hocks (ham)
2 medium potatoes
2 medium carrots (1 cup)
2 stalks of celery (1 cup)
1 medium onion
¾ teaspoon thyme
½ teaspoon salt
¼ teaspoon pepper
Makes 8 to 10 servings.

PEA SOUP
2 cups dried yellow peas
6 cups cold water
1 medium chopped onion
¾ to 1 pound pork hocks

Soak peas in water overnight, and then drain. In a 3 quart pot, cover peas with 6 cups of water. Bring to a boil. Skim off any pea husks that rise to the surface. Add the chopped onion, ½ teaspoon thyme, and pork. Bring to a boil. Lower heat and simmer with pot covered for about 1 to 1 ½ hours. Season with salt. I use a bag of dried yellow peas–takes more water. Then I add a good ½ cup of finely chopped celery and carrots.

Life on the prairies had its ups and downs. In some years, wheat yielded 45 bushels an acre and in others, barely 15. Some years the hot prairie winds would destroy the crops, especially when the grain was in the milk. When this grain was harvested the kernels would be small and dry, giving a low yield. Then there were hailstorms and windstorms, dry years and wet years.

The most dreaded of all were grasshoppers. I made many trips to the Cedoux elevator to get loads of poisoned bran. Dad, Daniel, and I would shovel this bran around the fields.

Grasshoppers would eat this bran and die. Dead grasshoppers laid inches deep around the fields. When rain was scarce there were grasshoppers, it seemed they came with drought. When rain was plentiful–the mosquitoes came by the hordes, making life miserable for man and beast. Special string harnesses and nose baskets were worn on the horses to ward off the pests. The prairie winds helped during the day, which kept them from flying. When the winds died down in the evening, they came in swarms. August taught the children how to make smudge pots. Dry grass or straw was placed in the bottom of a heavy bucket. Then as the fire burned, green grass and manure were added. Lots of smoke was created by this and smoldered into the night. These were placed in the doorways of the barn and smoke wafted through the barn making it possible for the horses to eat their oats and hay in peace and then lay down to rest.

In the summer time when storms developed during the day, we were ordered out of the house and to crawl into the wild rose bushes and stay there until the storm passes. When storms came at night, Mom covered the table with a big blanket. The children crawled under the table so they would not see the lightening, which frightened them.

It seemed the wind was God. It had so much control with the crops, drying clothes, blizzards and pollination. The waving, golden ripening wheat fields appeared like liquid gold. The blooming flax fields looked like waves on a blue lake. The wind also had its finger in the lining up the belt with the steam engine.

In the wintertime, the prevailing wind was from the North or Northwest. Straw stacks formed a shelter and food on the leeward side for horse and hogs. Chickens huddled on their roosts in the hen house. Two teams of horses and two cows were kept in the barn. The horse could chew on snow for water, but the snow was melted for the cows and the family. The hens did not lay eggs, as the hen house was not insulated.

School was called off when it was below zero weather and windy. Children had a difficult time getting home, as horses rebel at heading into the wind.

After Florence was born Dad bought a three-quarter section of land for eight dollars an acre. There was a house on this property which Dad, with help, raised the roof that made bedrooms. Here the girls, boys, and parents each had a bedroom. Florence and I had the Southwest one with a window. This was a nice home including a telephone and two chimneys. No central heat here either, in the winter everything froze. This place had a cellar where produce from the garden and other things including dad's beer was kept. Our source of water, the well, froze up too. This was our last home in Saskatchewan, no trees here either.

Dad bought a piano and I took piano lessons from Mrs. Bierma who lived in Cedoux. This musical training included eleven lessons, which I took during summer vacation. When I didn't ride horseback to my lessons, I ran through the wheat fields to Mrs. Bierma's. The times that I ran to my lessons, my clothes would be wet so I would hang them out on the clothesline while I took my piano lessons. I prefered horse-back riding since I was afraid of the coyotes. One can never image all the pleasures I have had playing piano.

After Dad purchased this section of land it was necessary to have hired help. He still rented the half section from Dr. Allen. Joe and Martin, both bachelors, were of Polish descent and were the two men hired. Joe was the first one hired. He was a very nice man and we loved him. He was Catholic and attended services north of Cedoux. He often jokingly told about stopping and getting a supply of holy water from one of the sloughs on his way.

One day Mom found Joe lying on the ground by the water trough. He was unconscious and bleeding profusely from a hole in his head. A horse had kicked him. She applied cold clothes on his wound and washed away the dirt while waiting for Dr. Allen. After putting in some stitches, Dr. Allen left medicine and instructions for my Mother who took care of him. Joe went back to Poland that year.

Martin was a smaller man and spoke broken English. My dad was very strict with his help and had less patience with him than Joe. It seemed Martin would complain to Mom, she always listened, understood and gave comfort. One such time he must have scolded him severely as Martin, close to crying, confessed to Mom "August he gimming me hell for throwing the horse over the fence mit some hay." Hired help slept in the bunkhouse and ate their meals with the family. Martin went to work for another farmer and once when Dad and Mom visited him, he confided in Lily how much he missed her. Particularly, how now he had to do his own laundry, which he had to do on Sundays.

MAGIC PAN BASIC CREPES
1 cup shifted flour
½ teaspoon salt
3 eggs
1 ½ sups milk
1 tablespoon melted butter
(I use more butter so I don't oil the pan for each crepe)

The year my Dad started the beef ring was exciting and interesting. A group of wheat farmers had a meeting to decide whether to start a beef ring. The idea of the ring was that if each farmer donated a beef animal of equal size, they could have fresh meat. This brought about many questions, e.g. who would butcher the animal, where would the butchering take place, and on and on. Some argued in Polish, others in Swedish. My Dad volunteered to do the butchering of the animal at his farm in return for a share of the meat without having to supply an animal. It was agreed.

In preparation for this, he built a new granary, dug a deep hole to dispose of the blood and intestines, etc. Then each farmer was given a number, which was displayed, in the granary above the spike that would hold his meat. A large map or picture of a beef carcass was hung on the wall showing all the different cuts of meat of the whole carcass. An animal a week—by the end of the summer season each farmer would have received a whole carcass, having a different piece each week.

Each Friday, an animal would arrive at our farm in the afternoon. Dad had constructed a tripod with a block and tackle arranged over the slaughtering area. The animal was held fast by a halter and nose ring that was fastened to a dead bolt. After the animal was shot, the blood drained into the designated hole and the block and tackle pulled the animal up into a hanging position above the ground. By slitting the stomach area open, removing the innards, which disappeared into the deep hole, the wench would then lift the animal higher so wild animals couldn't get at it. It hung there for a couple hours to cool. In the late evening, some help would come and the animal was taken down and placed on a long sturdy table in the granary where Dad would skin it and with his trusty meat saw would cut it into the different cuts of meat.

In the morning each piece was put into a sturdy white numbered bag and hung on the spike with the corresponding number. By the end of the butchering season each farmer had received each cut of meat including liver and heart. In 1925 no one had any form of refrigeration so the meat was eaten before the end of the week. Fresh meat was a real treat and this way no one had to travel far, as it was a great distance to a butcher shop. It was a neighborhood venture and served the purpose well.

Our farm had a very deep well where ice formed in a ring and remained nearly all summer. Our share of the meat was put in a container and lowered by rope down to rest on the ice. By storing it this way, my Mother didn't have to bake it all at once, only as needed. Needless to say, Dan, Rudy and

I ran home from school on Fridays to watch this butchering event and to help where needed. I also helped by playing with Florence while my Mother helped Dad with all the bookwork this undertaking created.

SWEDISH HASH
1 large onion, hopped
2 tablespoons butter
2 cups diced cooked beef or pork
4 to 6 medium sized potatoes cooked
Salt and pepper to taste
*   I used to use a meat grinder to grind it all up. In a large heavy skillet sauté onion in butter. Add meat, potatoes, salt, and pepper. Cook until mixture is lightly browned. Sprinkle with parsley. Serve with fried eggs and pickled beets. Makes 4 to 6 servings.*

We used a round tub for Saturday night bath time— imagine how much snow it would take to make several gallons of water in the wintertime. Until Florence arrived, I was always first, because we were girls. The boys last—no change of water. Hot water was added as needed. Mom and Dad bathed in the same water after the children were in bed and asleep. The used clothing was then put into the tub to soak and washed on laundry day.

We each had a change of clothing. In the winter; long legged and long sleeved fleece lined underwear with a drop seat, black long stockings, pants and shirts for the boys— navy serge dress for and two aprons for me. Most of the outerwear was worn for weeks, washed only if dirty, especially in the wintertime. Laundry was done on a washboard with a of bar soap. The laundry was hung out to freeze dry and then hung up in the house on lines strung across the rooms. In the spring and summer it was hung on lines outside. Very often the prairie winds were so strong the laundry was not hung out until they died down, or hung out early before it got windy.

Although Dad used swear words, he was very strict with

us; no one else in the home could swear or there would be harsh punishment. On one occasion the family were all sitting at the table eating dinner, repeating words that rhymed. I said "teapot" Daniel burst out with "peepot". The words were hardly out of his mouth when August hit him in the mouth knocking out two teeth. Another time when Mom and Dad were expecting dinner guests, I stood up in the window, looking west to see if they were on their way "those #*&%# people have not left yet." Dad jerked me out of the window, placed me across his lap—the lashes with his leather belt were unbearable. Mother pleaded, "August have mercy".

I crawled under the bed and hung onto the bedsprings. Dad pushed the bed around, trying to dislodge me, yelling "you get out from under there or you will get more of the same treatment." I never did obey that command. Every time for several weeks when he entered the house, I crawled under the bed. He finally forgot about it, that was the first and last lashing I ever received. I never disobeyed him, or swore again; regardless what he asked, demanded or ridiculed me about. It was hard for my Mother to accept his strong discipline of raising children.

Children were to be seen and not heard.

During the 1920s my Grandmother, Anna, wrote many letters to Lily. She was worried about her husband's health. He visited doctors often and was diagnosed as having cancer with no hope for survival. She pleaded with Lily to come and visit her step-dad, who also was August's uncle. August and Lily decided to go to Minnesota and spend the month of July 1928. Lily wrote Anna that as soon as school was out and I wrote my eighth grade exams, they would come. School was out the last week of June. I had to write my exams by July first. I rode several miles on horseback to the school where the exams were written in thirteen subjects. Later when I received a telegram from Saskatoon Saskatchewan announcing I had graduated with honors from the eighth grade; to me this was quite something—almost unbelievable.

The whole family was excited about taking a trip to Minnesota. We would meet our grandma and meet cousins. Lily would see her mother after fourteen years and August his dying uncle. The only relative we had ever seen was Uncle Otto, Dad's brother. He had made two visits to Cedoux coming from British Columbia. Otto worked for the railroad so he traveled by train. I always thought he was stingy since he would bring two candy bars, one for Daniel and Rudy and none for me.

The day of departure for Minnesota finally arrived. Mother had everything packed including a big lunch. Dad had to stop in Weyburn and buy beer. They stopped and ate lunch on the way to North Portal, where they would go through customs. This was quite an experience. It seemed like the car and luggage were x-rayed—they went through everything. As they crossed the border into North Dakota, Dad started chuckling. As thoroughly as the customs officers searched everything, they did not find the bottle of beer he had hidden in the upholstery in the back seat. We spent the first night in a hotel in northern North Dakota by a lake. This was the first time we children had stayed in a hotel or had seen a lake.

Bright and early the next day we were on our way. The road signs (an Indian face) were posted on the telephone poles. The gravel roads were dusty and wash boardy. In the afternoon a threatening black cloud was forming and developing fast. Dad drove off the road seeking shelter by a high bank. Hurriedly the side curtains were snapped on the McGlocklin Buick touring car to keep us from getting wet. The rain fell in torrents with lightening flashing and lots of thunder, but no hail. Water was running in the ditch. When Dad tried to get back on the road, the car was stuck. A farmer came by and his team pulled the car back on the road. We stayed in a hotel in Valley City and finished eating the food in the lunch basket. After a bath, all were happy getting cleaned up and anxious to get to bed and have a good night rest–we were all tired. Tomorrow we would reach our destination and see the Millie Lacs Lake that Mother had told us so much about.

We all awoke early, and after a good breakfast of all the pancakes they could eat, they were on their way headed for Brunswick, Minnesota. We children could hardly believe our eyes at the size of Millie Lacs Lake. "That looks as big as an ocean," exclaimed Rudy. Dad soon put us straight describing the Atlantic Ocean he had crossed coming to North America. We also remarked about all the trees, rivers and smaller lakes on the way.

We arrived at Grandma Anna's home in daylight. My mother wept with joy as she hugged and kissed her mother, who was much heavier than she was fourteen years ago. We met our Aunt Bertha and Uncle Hilding, both older than me. Grandma had such a beautiful two-story gingerbread home with sixty acres about a half-mile east of Brunswick. The downstairs consisted of a large kitchen, a large living room, a downstairs bedroom and an open porch to the south. A stairway led to the upstairs with two big bedrooms and a smaller one at the landing of the stairs. She also had what she called a "summer kitchen" and an outdoor toilet, a small barn, and a well with a pump on it. In the summer months all the laundry, cooking, baking, canning and soap making were done in this "summer kitchen". They even ate their meals there—thus the house was kept clean, odorless and cool.

Grandmother's kitchen had three filmy curtained windows to let in the afternoon sun. A door to the south and another to the north regulated the temperature, especially in the hot summer. In the hot summer both doors were left open to let in the breezes. During the winter months the south door remained closed. The north or entry door, during the cold months, had a worn rolled up rug at the bottom to keep out the draft of the cold wind. The worn white pine floor was scrubbed weekly with P and G soap. The shiny black and nickel trimmed wood burning stove stood near the east wall between the living room door and the pantry door. A large chipped wood box, near the stove, always needed filling. A square oak table, six straight backed chairs, treadle sewing machine, kerosene lamp, a wall clock and rocking chair completed the furniture in her kitchen.

I seem to remember grandma's kitchen the best. Maybe it's because of all the wonderful things she made in the kitchen. One of my favorite times was when she would make bread. When a child walks into her kitchen after school and smells the tantalizing fragrance of homemade bread, he knows he is in luck. The odor of baking bread causes ones olfactory senses released and one is instantly hungry. Spreading fresh butter on a warm slice of bread is so satisfying; the true meaning of good eating.

Grandmother always used potato water and a cup of mashed potato for the liquid in her bread recipe. Using her favorite right sized crock, she added a nail hard yeast cake that dissolved slowly in the lukewarm liquid. This covered crock was placed in the warming oven of the stove. Each time wood was fed to the stove this liquid was stirred to help dissolve the yeast. When we, the three of us, arrived from school the yeasty odor alerted us that Grandmother would be baking bread the next day.

Our DeLaval cream separator in the pantry was used twice daily to separate milk. As the warm milk gushed out of the long spout into a galvanized tub, thick foam formed at the top. Here Grandmother stood with her large wooded bowl and ladle, scooping up the foam to add to her liquid, which she declared made her bread light and airy. About one half of the required amount of flour was stirred into the liquid mixture. Grandma stirred until it was smooth and the gluten was released. Kneading the remaining flour into the dough relieves frustrations and is good therapy. Kneading yeast breads develops this protein (gluten) stretched by yeast, and makes the loaves' framework. Grandmother used her fingers by inserting one finger a half-inch into the dough, if the indentation remained, the dough had doubled and was ready to be baked. She used her thermometer arm to test the oven for the right temperature to bake her bread. Bread making is an art; but in grandmother's kitchen, making six perfectly shaped loaves from the oven truly was a miracle.

SWEDISH RYE BREAD

1 package yeast
¼ cup molasses
1 ½ cups hot water
2 tablespoons grated orange peel
¼ cup warm water
1 tablespoon salt
2 1/2 cups stirred medium rye flour
3 1/2 to 4 cups shifted flour
¼ cup brown sugar
2 tablespoons shortening

Soften yeast in warm water. In big bowl combine sugar, molasses, salt and shortening. Add hot water and stir until sugar dissolves. Cool. Stir in rye flour and beat well. Add softened yeast and orange rind. Mix well. Stir in enough flour to make a soft dough. Cover let rest 10 minutes. Knead on a well-floured surface until smooth. Place dough in lightly greased bowl, turn once to grease surface. Cover let rise in warm place until double (1/2 to 2 hours). Punch down, divide into 2 portions and put in round pans let rise until double. Bake in moderate oven at 375 degrees for about 30 minutes. Makes 2 loaves.

Grandmother's driveway was lined with large shady oaks on both sides. There were many large shade trees in the yard. The tree closest and east of the house had a swing tied to one of its branches. We three older children enjoyed the swing (a new thing in our lives). It reminded me of a favorite poem—"Oh, how I love to go up in a swing", by Robert L. Stevenson.

My brothers and I spent most of this vacation with our aunt and uncle and their two sons, who lived in Spring Vale. Vacation Bible school was offered there at a small Baptist church. It was a great experience for us as we never attended Sunday school. We all helped with the chores, picking strawberries, haying, milking cows and housework. In the evening we swam in the Rum River. One Sunday a picnic was planned. We all (two carloads) went to the Minnehaha Park. Hiawathas' poem came alive as we watched the falls and touched the statues. To us, Minnesota was such a beautiful place.

In fact this trip changed all of our lives. Due to grandfather's illness (he would pass away in September of 1928), my grandmother encouraged my parents to buy her sixty-acre farm. Mom and Dad decided to sell their property when they returned to Saskatchewan. In late summer we took a trip to Regina, eighty miles, to apply for immigration to the United States. I had been sick for several days with Scarlitina, and my face was red and swollen. The appointment could not be broken, so papers were filed and pictures were taken. Needless to say my picture was awful. It was rather a scary experience as everything was so formal. Evidently the authorities were satisfied, as immigration papers were granted to immigrate to the United States of America.

In the late fall of 1928 my feelings about many things kept me awake nights. Especially was this true the day of the auction. It seemed everything was coming to a close. The day of the farm auction was a busy one. The family spent a good hour making sandwiches and filling a bag lunch for all attending the auction. It was not a happy day.

The hardest to see go was the pet dog, a coyote and collie crossbred. I begged Dad to let me ride my buckskin pony, May, to Minnesota, but his answer was a definite "NO". I cried when she was sold. I loved that horse. She was my transportation, my recreation. I spent hours upon hours on her warm back. "Going, going, gone—SOLD." I heard the auctioneer say. She was tied behind a car with her teammate, Nancy on their way to a new home near Moose Jaw.

I was in my mid-teens. It was exciting to think of moving to the land of my mother's birth, but on the other hand I thought "will I ever see the Wickstroms again, especially their nephew, Ernest. Would I ever see the Browns, the Katt family, all dear friends, classmates, and neighbors. This day left an indelible note in my mind, because at fifteen I knew that friends and intangible things would be left here on the prairie that I knew and loved, but would never be forgotten. After the auction everything that was left of living fourteen years in southern Saskatchewan was packed in a few trunks. We left that night on a train, immigrating to Brunswick, Minnesota.

MINNESOTA

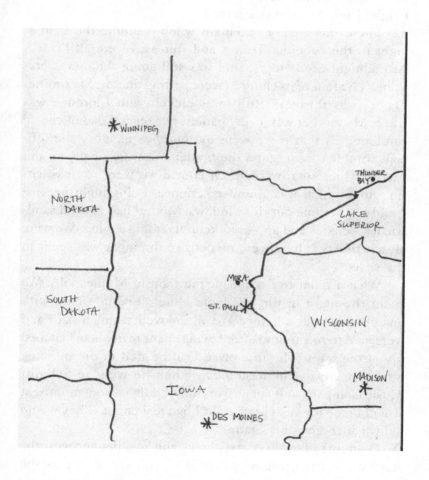

We were to leave Weyburn by train—destination North Portal. After the auction we went to Weyburn and Dad bought all of us new coats—the first purchased outer garments we had ever had. Then dinner at a Greek restaurant and later boarded the train at eight o'clock for North Portal. When asked by the waiter what they wanted to drink, Florence at two years of age said, "baby wants some beer". Dad laughed but Mom was stunned.

There was much excitement when boarding the train at eight in the evening. Trunks and suitcases were all loaded. At midnight the border patrol was still going through everything. The four of us children were getting uneasy. My brother Daniel was thirteen, Rudy was eleven, and Florence was three. My mother was a very patient person and dad of course cautioned us that if we were too noisy or naughty the officials wouldn't let us cross the border. We were finally on our way to Minnesota by train. Of course we were restless, sitting up all night was a new experience. Being nighttime we could see nothing out the windows. Mother had packed sandwiches, cookies and apples to keep us from starving. We were always thirsty. There were no beds so the night was spent in the seats.

What a relief to disembark the train in Minneapolis. We spent the night in the Vendome Hotel. Taking a bath with lots of water was a luxury. We all enjoyed taking a bath and were able to run around after having spent many hours cooped up on the train. The first place Dad headed in the morning was a garage to purchase a car. Then he went to Schmitt Music Company and spent five hundred dollars on an upright Grand Piano for me. He thought I had real talent. They would deliver it to grandma's farm.

Grandma's farm was sixty-acres and was bought with the agreement that grandma would live with us as long as she lived. Grandmother had eleven cows and three horses, all old, and chickens. Of the three horses, "Skip", a younger gelding, was my favorite. I definitely disliked all the fences and gates! The other horses were old and one had the heaves.

Getting acquainted with all the children in the neighborhood was hilarious. Every evening up to twelve young people got together and played all kinds of games. All lived within a quarter mile of each other. Getting back to school was quite scary. We Canadians with different pronunciation of words caused some laughter among the students. The three room Brunswick School was only a half-mile away. The boys had gone to school all fall in Saskatchewan and I had started the ninth grade in November. I had my graduation with honors certificate from the eighth grade with me so the suspicious lady teacher was satisfied.

I had made friends with Maxine who had a riding pony. We both rode Lady bareback. Our ninth grade teacher, a lady, thought this form of locomotion was unlady like. I don't think she ever liked me—the feeling was mutual. My brothers and I were all great students, so we were accepted that way. I just couldn't get Algebra. I got a passing grade—however, I had a hard time accepting that.

Ninth graders had to finish the last six weeks of school in Mora. I never did get algebra. After the first Algebra test Mr. Larson saw my trouble and said he would tutor me after school. This meant I had a seven-mile walk or run home each night, which I was glad to do. Those days one had to take tests to advance to a higher grade. Thanks to Mr. Larson I passed with the highest grade of the class in Algebra. Needless to say I took all the math and science classes that he taught. He was the best, most patient teacher I ever had.

FRIED OATMEAL COOKIES
2 cups brown sugar
1 cup lard or shortening
2 eggs
4 cups oatmeal
Pinch of salt

1 ½ cups flour
1 level teaspoon baking soda
1 teaspoon baking powder
Take half the lard and place in frying pan, put in the oatmeal and fry. Then add the sugar, eggs, and rest of the shortening. Drop by spoonful onto a baking sheet and bake in oven (350 degrees) until light brown.

It was the summer of 1929 and I had joined a Gospel Group. On Sunday afternoons members of the group went to other churches to attend the young peoples meetings. Our group sang songs (solos, trios etc) and gave testimonies about our faith and love of God. Much like my missionary work with my mother in Saskatchewan, I was very dedicated to this group. One particular Sunday I was quite excited. Grandma Anna had ordered a new dress for me. I was to wear this pretty dress on this very special day-my baptismal day.

I was to pack a white nightgown and a few petticoats and meet at the first house on the left after crossing the twin bridges on Highway 11. When we arrived at this house we were ushered in and listened to a short service. We took off all our clothing and put on the petticoats and nightgown; we were eleven of us girls. We walked on the road, crossed the bridge and then off the road to the right and down to the river on the bank of the Snake River.

I was baptized by immersion. I wasn't the first one. There were several people on the bridge watching this event. These people were parents, brothers, sisters, other relatives and friends. Some making it a laughing stock some praying, some swearing. It took a lot of courage to be baptized not being carried by loving arms like when babies are baptized. With a deep commitment to become a child of God, I walked into the hip deep water and the pastor dipped me backward into the water three times. "I baptize you in the name of the Father ("hold your nose and don't swallow"), in the name of the

Son (dunked again), and in the name of the Holy Spirit (dunked again), Amen".

My clothes clung to me and when we had all been baptized we walked back across the bridge and into the house to dry off and get back into my new dress. I didn't even think about how my hair looked. I was a child of God and so happy to have let Christ into my heart. My Grandma and my mother were Baptist. My Dad at that time didn't believe in God but didn't object to my decision to be baptized. Dad had been baptized as an infant in Sweden and confirmed too; but at this time I was baptized he mocked Christianity at Sunday evening Services. He was one of the men we prayed for.

Most teenagers, at that time and now, have a problem with drinking, sex etc., but my trouble was with religion. I believed in the Bible and the love of God, but had trouble interpreting parts of it. Most likely if I had had the opportunity of attending Sunday School and other formal study it would have been easier for me to grasp.

Train up a child in the way he should go,
and he will not depart from it.

My junior year in school was sad and disappointing. One night in January 1930, I overheard my parents arguing about whether to have a child born in Minnesota. My mother very definitely did not want another child—four was enough. She became pregnant anyway. Her attitude did not change and she remarked several times that she was unhappy about being pregnant. Her birthday was August 8, she turned thirty-seven. Some of the neighbor ladies came with gifts and cake. Mother remarked afterwards that she would have no use of the gifts.

"Mom, you can make yourself three pretty dresses out of these materials" I said. "Which do you like the best?" Her reply was that I could have them or if I didn't like them I should give them to grandma.

My Aunt Selma asked the family over for dinner the following Sunday. Selma liked to read tea leaves, as she often did after drinking tea with desert—strawberry shortcake. When the cups were empty, they were turned upside down on the saucer. When Selma read mother's cup she said, "I see a lot of tears." No one paid much attention as all the cups were read as fun.

Mother did not have any prenatal care. Her appetite was poor. She was sad but continued to care for her family and lame mother. She had done some laundry the day she gave birth. In the evening she sat in the corner chair in the kitchen. At bedtime she remarked, "When I go to bed tonight I don't think I will ever get out of it." A three-pound boy was born that night, October 22; a doctor from Mora was present.

The morning of November 1, 1930 Mother had a stroke— Mary from across the road and I were with her. She could not speak, but her mouth was drawn down. A registered nurse was called to come and care for her. She suffered the second stroke in the early afternoon, the nurse declared it serious. The family was eating supper when the nurse came down and announced that Mother had suffered another stroke and was dead. Dad rushed upstairs to see; she was truly dead— gone. The mortician from Braham was called. They carried her down in a basket.

Dad ran and screamed amid the rows of driveway trees. We children sought comfort with Mary. Everyone was crying and wringing their hands—they were stunned. After a day or so the mortician brought Mom home in a casket and placed it in the living room. He opened the lid or cover and there she lay for a few days until the funeral—November fifth. Neighbors and friends came to sit and pay last respects—some brought food.

My Grandmother's heart was broken again, "why must I endure all these tragedies? Peter and John, my husbands, Alida, Harry, Gottfred, Agnes and now my first born only thirty-seven years old. She left five children, this last one cries all the time." Grandma Anna lived to be eighty-six and was of great comfort to we five children while she lived.

At that time Daniel was fifteen, Rudy thirteen, Florence nearly six and I had just turned seventeen. Grandma, Florence and I stayed with Dad. Dan and Rudy were home awhile that winter. My grandmother was deaf and had fallen earlier and broken her hip. After a stay at Braham hospital she came home very lame, but managed to get around with the help of a cane. Harold cried all the time. Grandma couldn't hear him cry–and I had very little sleep. Early to bed and early to rise was a kept rule in the home. Milking cows, cleaning the barn, hauling cream to the creamery, housework was endless. Friday and Saturday nights we could be up until ten. I liked going to bed before eight and getting up at five, this was the routine I was used to. I loved grandma dearly, but raising Harold had to end. Dad made some arrangement with Aunt Sally and Harold ended up living with Aunt Sally and Uncle Gust before Christmas, which made life somewhat easier.

Dad spoiled Florence; I suppose she was an out for him. However, it seemed that Florence was always naughty and of course Dad was more of a disciplinarian than before. It wasn't easy for him either, to be left with an old lame grandma and five children. Then, in February 1931 Dad lost most of his right foot in a wood cutting accident at Larms so I had to quit school that year. My dream of being a math teacher vanished. Maxine quit school when I did—at the time of mother's death. Maxine and her mother were family for my brothers and I.

In the fall of 1931, I begged to go back to school. Dad gave consent only if I got all the chores done in the morning and for the day including getting the cream to the creamery. By going to bed early and rising early I did just fine. Grandma and I laundered on Saturday and baked up for the week. Florence only had a half-mile to school, which was just past the creamery. The school bus left the store at 7:30 a.m. and I made it every day.

We all lived here until Dan and Rudy finished the eighth grade. My brothers left home as soon as they graduated from the eighth grade. Dan went to work on a dairy farm in Maiden Rock, Wisconsin and later Rudy lived with Mrs. Fritchie and helped her with chores and fieldwork, as she was a widow.

Rural schools at that time gave programs at Christmas Time. This was great entertainment including lunches. Each school trying to have a better program than the one before. It was at one of these Christmas programs that I met Carl Ericksen. I rode with Dan and his girlfriend to the Christmas program at the three-room school in Brunswick. Then this good-looking well-dressed man came in and sat by Dan. He recognized Dan because Dan had helped fill silos for the

Ericksens. Carl started a conversation with Dan and found out that I was his sister. I didn't flirt and he respected my evasiveness and could see that I trusted Dan. Maybe I was different from the ladies he had dated before. In fact he had been engaged to one of my classmate's sisters.

When the program and lunch was over the four of us went out to the car to go home. Carl had followed us out and got in to the back seat. I was in the front seat with Dan and Vivian. "Hilda, would you like to go to the Coin school program with me", asked Carl. "I will", I answered, "if Dan goes along". Dan agreed, it was decided we would all go and we did.

Dan went along for several dates. Carl was so well dressed, white shirt and necktie and a hat. He was so handsome. He didn't smoke either. He was all of six feet tall and broad shouldered. He knew that Dan and I had lost our mother, I'm sure I was still mourning her death.

On Christmas Eve day, I worked for a couple in Brunswick preparing Christmas Eve dinner. (My mother had worked for these people when she was young). I was to be there at noon, eat before coming, and stay until dinner was served and dishes done. They ate at the groaming board table and I ate in the kitchen. A groaming board is a table loaded with food. While I watched the kettles cooking, they were telephoning all their relatives wishing them a Merry Christmas. I was done before nine and while putting on my jacket I received twenty-five cents. Believing I had to walk the half a mile home, I was very surprised to see Carl parked outside to take me home. Dad must have told him where I was. He came inside and presented me with a Christmas present. It was a lovely box of stationary. I finally went alone with Carl because he just kept asking.

Dad must have liked Carl as he consented to let me date him. He could come on Wednesday nights and when I went to bed, he played checkers with my dad. When Saturday night came there he was. We visited his friends. They played cards and at that time I didn't because of my Baptist affiliation, it was a sin, so was dancing and movies. Carl was Lutheran.

After attending church with Carl a few times, I began to realize that Lutherans were not going to hell as I had been told. Carl never criticized my faith he accepted me as I was even if I was so confused. I trusted him and looked forward to our dates, understand he was nearly six years older than me (he wasn't a kid). Each time he came he gave me a roll of lifesavers and dimes now and then so I could buy a bowl of soup when I went to school. I loved him. Somehow I felt safe with him and his parents. Carl started stopping at the school when he was in town. Sometimes at noon hour, I would go out and visit with him. Some of the young men that I knew only wanted to kiss etc.–which I didn't like to do; I was more interested in getting an education. I still wanted to be a Math teacher.

When Carl took me to meet his parents for the first time it was scary for me. Hans and Sena were definitely Danish. I liked them immediately. I didn't hesitate when Carl asked me to sing for them. "Let the rest of the world go by" was his suggestion.

Carl kept me feeling odd as he bragged about what a good singer I was, also remarking about my beautiful black hair. I waited for him to talk about my sparkling brown eyes. Hans and Sena enjoyed my singing—they applauded.

LET THE REST OF THE WORLD GO

Is the struggle and strife
We find in this life
Really worth while after all
I've been wishing today
I could just run away
Out where the west winds call
With someone like you
A pal good and true

I'd like to leave it all behind,
And go and find
Some place that's known
To God alone
Just a spot to call our own
We'll find perfect peace
Where joys never cease
Out there beneath a kindly sky
We'll build a sweet little nest
Somewhere in the West
And let the rest of the world go by

Sena was a tall and plump lady with arthritis. Hans was shorter than Sena and not very big. He wore a mustache and smoked a pipe. I could tell Sena wore the pants in the family, but had no control over Carl. They invited me for Sunday dinner after going with them to the Lutheran Church. I helped milk the cows in the evening before Carl took me home, milked our cows and was in bed by eight o'clock. Carl would stay and play checkers with my Dad. Neither Carl or Dad had to get up in the morning—I had to have the cows milked, chores done, cream to the creamery and on the bus by 7:30 a.m.

It was easy to direct people to the Stone Porch Ericksens. This Stone Porch house was one of a kind situated four miles south of Mora, Minnesota on Highway 65. It was sixty-five miles north of Minneapolis and one hundred miles south of Duluth. In innumerable ways it has remained the same.

An old-timer of twenty years hence would miss seeing Hans and Sena sitting on the porch or in the rather large kitchen. Hans usually sat in his comfortable rocker and Sena in hers; both had their feet warming on the oven door. At intervals Hans would lay his book aside to feed the "monster" and Sena busily knitted heavy wool socks and mittens while reading the Danish "Quinden och Hjommet". They occasionally conversed in Danish discussing their daily labor and community affairs. Their only son Carl, would never grow up and was often criticized for walking to the neighbors to play Karems and eat cake and homemade ice cream.

Stone Porch Ericksens settled in Mora in 1915, having lived previously in Southern Iowa ,after immigrating from their beloved Denmark. They came to live in this rich new land as sweethearts and were married in 1904. They decided to give it a few more years before they would return to their native land. When arriving by train from Iowa with their possessions of household furnishings and horses, their first acquaintance was a friendly Irishman married to a Swede, whose hospitality was unique and gracious. Little did Hans, Sena, and seven year old Carl know at the time that they would remain.

Hans and Sena's wedding picture

One of the times that Carl met me for lunch at school was on March 12, 1932. We took a short ride on Highway 23, east of Mora. He pulled over to the side of the road by some pine trees and opened a small box and presented me with a diamond ring. He told me that he loved me and had never met such a lovely Christian girl and wanted me for his wife. I couldn't believe that any man could love this skinny (ugly girl I thought) with beautiful black hair and shining brown eyes. I accepted the ring and said I'd think about marriage for a couple of days. On March 14th, Carl's tewnty-fourth birthday, I said yes.

During this time, Dad started going over to Gullicksons regularly to play cards. It wasn't long before card playing was not the only attraction. The Gullickson guys have a sister, Selma, a school friend of moms, the same age and unmarried. Once in awhile when dad come home from a date with Selma, he would come into Florence and my bedroom and check my feet to see if they were cold and that I never broke the Saturday night curfew.

When Carl and I told Dad we were going to be married in July, he put the farm up for sale. His farmerette was leaving– getting married in July. It was sold to the Westbergs in June. We moved to a beautiful, big, vacant farmhouse with hardwood floors southwest of Brunswick, just Dad, grandma, Florence and I. The wedding reception was held here for about forty guests. July first was the last night I spent there. It was hard to leave Grandma and Florence.

Carl said that I could still go to school and graduate. I was so glad that there was never any pressure for sex. I don't think I could have handled that. He told everyone that I was his French Canadian Indian. I had not been feeling too good with pain in my stomach area. When I complained to Dad his reaction was "uh huh been playing around huh?" Assuming I was pregnant. I didn't see a Doctor. When I told Carl he took me to his doctor and I was diagnosed with gall bladder trouble and anemia so I got medicine for that.

Carl and Hilda's wedding picture

I married Carl on July 2, 1932 at the Brunswick Lutheran Church at two p.m. I had finished my junior year in High School. In those days newlyweds were treated to a chivarie. A chivarie was a gathering of neighbors and friends at the place where the newlyweds were staying. The group would usually arrive after dark and make lots of noise–banging pots, pans, kettles, and saws–until the newlyweds came out and took them out for a treat. On our wedding night, Carl treated all the noisemakers with homemade ice cream, cookies, candy, and cigars. He kept a close eye on me since it was also common for the bachelors to steal the bride for a ransom.

It was after midnight when we got back home to the Ericksen farm. We were very tired. Carl's parents had told us we could sleep in on Sunday morning. We would all go to the eleven o'clock service in Brunswick. When we threw back the sheets to go to bed we found the sheets sewed down to the mattress. A bushel or more of pinecones were between the sheets!!! My Aunt Sally and a neighbor lady were guilty of that prank.

This salad was served at my wedding, which I made and was stored in the creamery:

PARADISE PUDDING
1 package lemon Jell-O
2 cups boiling water
½ cup blanched almonds
12 marshmallows
12 cherries
6 macaroons
4 tablespoons of sugar
¼ teaspoon salt
1 cup of cream whipped.

Dissolve the Jell-O in the boiling water then chill. When slightly thickened, beat until thick like cream. Mix nuts, marshmallows, cherries, wafers, sugar, salt together in a bowl. Add Jell-O. Fold in whipped cream. Chill until firm. Serve in slices.

Two days later was the Fourth of July. A picnic was held at Ericksen's which included the neighborhood. A brother of Mr. Henning was visiting from Sweden. His name was Jonus. Every time he got near me he slapped my arm. I finally hauled off and kicked him in the hind-end. It hurt me too.

We (Carl, my brother Dan, and I) left on our honeymoon the next morning. Brother Dan and I were very close. The three of us had such a fun time going and coming to Saskatchewan. Carl had sixty-five dollars in cash. We stopped in Jamestown North Dakota to visit Carl's favorite Uncle Tony and Aunt Sofie. We spent a few days there and helped with farm work and had a good time. We told them we were going to Saskatchewan. Uncle Tony made us promise to stop again on our way home. They would have a barn dance in our honor. Carl and I would not have had it any other way.

On our honeymoon my big toe on my right foot started to get sore. In a few days it started to swell, got red and started to ache. When we got home, I went to the doctor and he sent me to the dentist as he thought something was causing the infection. The dentist said that the front gold tooth was abscessed and advised pulling it. The tooth came out and he gave me some pain pills to get some rest. I lain under a tree and took a long nap, as I hadn't slept well in a while. In a couple of days the swelling was down, the pain gone and the gold tooth was also gone. This started the beginning of false teeth. I had one false tooth on a denture for several years.

Dad remarried in December 1932 to Selma Gullickson, a dear friend of mother's who had never married. She had several brothers who played cards with dad. It took a few years for me to realize, accept, and finally love her dearly.

Lily's five children; Florence, Rudolph, Harold, Dan, Hilda

Yes, after I was married I did have an easier, happier life. I didn't have to get up so early, didn't have to go to bed at 7:30pm, and had more freedom. Our first six years of marriage was heavenly. But now you don't have to be told what happens when babies come—responsibility but very rewarding. *Whither thou goest, I will go; and where thou lodgest, I will lodge; thy people shall be my people, and thy God my God.* Ruth 1:16

I often think back to the first five years of my marriage to Carl. We lived with Carl's parents for over five years. Carl and his mother did a lot of arguing. She tried to control him, goodness he was twenty-four years old when we married. She ran the household and balanced the budget. In the early thirties, it took a very conservative person to make ends meet. The taxes were always paid and we had plenty to eat and enough work to keep us all busy.

Sena did the cooking, baking and helped with milking. Carl, nearly always, came late for milking, which always caused an argument. I loved to milk and feed calves. As soon as milking was done, Sena went to the house to make breakfast. Carl, Hans and I would remain to feed the animals. The milk was carried to the house where it was separated. At that time the cream was sold and the skim milk was fed to the hogs and chickens. The dog and cats got whole milk. Hans, Sena and Carl drank skim milk and Sena insisted I use whole milk because I was too thin.

In the spring, summer and fall there were crops to be put in, or to cultivate, haying and harvesting to do. I helped with all of it, and we all did gardening. We had all the vegetables we wanted. What we didn't eat fresh was canned in glass jars for future use. On raining days, Sena patched and sewed clothing. I did a lot of embroidering and crocheting. Carl and Hans would repair harnesses and take care of machinery.

June is dairy month and also haying time. As far back as I could remember Dad cut hay with a mower pulled by a team of horses. In Saskatchewan he didn't put up much hay. Enough was done to keep two cows and a team of horses over the winter months. In the late fall all the horses were let loose to fend for themselves until round up time in the Spring. Dad would pitch hay up into the barn loft and Dan and I would be up there in the heat pitching it back away from the door. In July it was so warm in the hayloft, our clothing would be wet with sweat.

When we moved to Minnesota in the late twenties, haying was done the same way. The alfalfa was cut by a horse-drawn mower. Then when it was dry enough I would sit on a dump rake pulled by a team of horses and every so many feet would pull a level and the hay would be dumped in a pile and proceed that way until all the hay was raked up. Then dad, the boys and I would put the hay in cocks using a three-tined fork. When this was finished the Haycocks were pitched unto the hayracks pulled by a team of horses. The barn was close to a shed and Dad said I was very good at getting a load of hay in there without hitting the barn or shed. The old method of pitching the hay into the loft with someone in the loft to pitch it back to the far wall was used. We were content when the loft was full and hay would hopefully last until spring. A few years later a rope sling was placed just so, and that eliminated all that pitching. A track placed near the roof and the length of the barn, where a sling full of hay was dumped and this replaced a lot of pitching.

The dump rack was replaced by a side rake, pulled by horse or a car. It placed the hay in long straight rows where a hay loader put the hay on the sling placed on the hayrack. Less pitching—easier work. Then came the hay baler—either round or square bales. Carl liked the round baler and it seemed that it was always the right time for baling during milking time. He liked to bale hay much more than milking. I would either drive the horses or the Ford tractor pulling the hay wagon from bale to bale. Then into the hayloft where they were piled neatly again. It was so hot in the hay loft. The water from the 120-foot well was so cold and refreshing.

All the different ways of haying have also been replaced

by haychoppers, which chopped up the hay and placed in silos called haylig. Small round and square bales have been replaced with elephant sized bales. Now these huge tractors are equipped with radios, televisions and air conditioning, you just have to know how to operate them. This is easier, more comfortable, a lot done in a short time; but something has been lost, the camaraderie is gone.

We had no trouble keeping the weight off. When evening came, chores and supper done, we hitched old Fleet Foot to the buggy and drove down to Snake River to cool off. Then climb into line dried sheets and sleep the hours away, refreshed and ready for another day to get that haying done before the fourth of July.

Picking the never ending rocks in spring and tons of potatoes in the fall and cutting a years supply of wood in the winter was routine. Popple would burn fast for quick heat, while elm, oak, and ash were used to bank the coals at night so that the house would stay warm for little Carl: still other kinds were used for smoking meat and fish.

After the land froze in early November, Carl and I spent hours in the woods. Uncle Tony owned forty acres north of the Bronson farm, which was heavily wooded. The agreement was as long as Sena paid the taxes, we could have all the wood we wanted. Carl and I would leave home in the dark and come home in the dark. We cut and trimmed trees all day. The wood was divided into lumber, and fence posts for heating. Red oak trees were very tough, but generally had a lot of leaves. The branches and twigs were piled and we often set fire to the brush piles to get warm and eat our frozen sandwiches, and make friends with the chickadees. In the wintertime the logs were placed on the sleigh and on the way home we unloaded the logs at the sawmill on the west side of Fish lake. We saved a few miles by crossing the lake when it was frozen.

We really enjoyed the winter months in the woods, listening to the birds, wind in the trees, chasing rabbits out of brush piles or just enjoying each other was a sharing that I will never forget. Carl and I could really handle that two man Swedish saw. We cut down some hardwood trees and some softwood trees. Carl trimmed out the hard wood and I did the softwood. The branches and twigs were neatly piled, the logs for lumber piled on the sleigh and the straight branches put in the post pile. The crooked and thinner branches piled for stove wood. We were a good team.

It was so nice to see the light of the home the last half-mile. Hans would put the team away and Sena had a warm supper, which we all enjoyed together. I don't think my feet were ever warm in the wintertime. When they did get warm after we were in bed awhile, they would itch just terrible. I had chill blaines, caused by nearly having frozen feet. In the late evening, I should say night we ate apples and cracked butternuts that grew on the east forty. About nine o'clock the hot water bottles were filled and placed in the upstairs bedrooms to take some of the cold out of the flannel sheets. I loved to cuddle up tot Carl to get warm. He always wore a stocking cap to bed. He had the worst sinus trouble and suffered a lot with it. He had dozen of things prescribed by doctors. It wasn't until late in life when we were not out in the cold anymore that he got relief.

Horse team with logs

Two never fail winter tasks were butchering and quilting. These were special. Oh, the enormous piles of wood and buckets of water, heated outdoors, were needed for butchering. No one could stick a hog or beef like the neighborly Irishman. Each neighbor helped the other and everything was saved but the squeal. The obnoxious sickening odor of cleaning the casings; the scary look of the boiled head and endless scraping of animal feet would amazingly turn into mouth watering sausage, silta and pickled pigs feet! Each neighbor was treated to a roast and part of the liver.

As necessary as it was for the men to get together for butchering; it was equally important that the ladies helped each other making quilts. Beautiful patched quilts filled with new wool tied just so with colorful yarn made excellent serviceable wedding gifts, if none were needed at home.

Hans and Sena often talked Danish to their Danish friends about me. After a couple of years I could understand a lot of what they were saying. At first I felt left out, as I understood very little and they always talked Danish when they had company. I could understand Swedish real well from my grandma, but this Danish was very different. Both Sena and Hans could sing. They were occasionally asked to sing at church, which they did. In the spring when Hans would be at the far end of the farm towards the river, the neighbors could hear him singing. Once in a great while Carl could hit a right note but most of the time he was monotone.

I often think of my in-law parents. I never got real close to Sena, I respected her, took her orders, but learned so much from her. She was so saving, she never wore out a whole dress. When the bodice got thin and full of holes, she put a new bodice on the still good skirt. Eventually the old skirt was replaced on the new bodice, the cycle went on and on. She was a tailor in her homeland, Denmark. When Carl was in grade school she had made him a winter jacket with tucks in the sleeves and jacket that she let out as needed. He was still wearing the jacket when we got married. She had the most beautiful complexion. Her face was washed every morning with soap and water. Her hair was reddish brown and worn in a large pug. I gave Sena her first hair cut when she couldn't raise her arms up anymore from arthritis. I really missed her when she died and realized then how I loved her and really never told her.

Hilda on horseback before kids

Before we had children, Carl got into the Insurance business. He was gone a lot, sometimes spending a week at a time away. Sena wasn't able to go to the barn anymore, so Hans and I spent many hours in the barns together especially in the wintertime. He was such gentleman and I thought the world of him. He was Sena's "go-for". Both he and Sena agreed that Carl had got himself a real good wife. As Sena got more crippled she finally let me do some cooking and baking. One year at Thanksgiving time she was bed ridden. We were expecting guests and she was somewhat upset that I would have to prepare the dinner. I don't think they thought I could cook, but I had taken over that job when my mother died. Anyway I received so many compliments that day that I should have gotten a big head. I could drive horses, milk cows, work in the garden, cook, bake, and sew.

For many years, at least five, we slept in the unheated upstairs. There were no storm windows on either. The northeast bedroom was closed off in the wintertime and served as a freezer for the meat. After butchering most of the meat was canned. What wasn't canned was kept in this room so you know how cold it was. Frost would form on all the upstairs windows up to half an inch thick. When the sun shone, we would hurriedly get upstairs and scrape the windows with a spatula before it fell on the floor and would leak onto the downstairs ceilings. Towels and rags were placed to absorb the drippings—it was a mess. We finally could afford to put on storm windows, there were eight windows upstairs.

In those early years in the wintertime we lived in the kitchen. The dining room and living room were closed off. There was a coal and wood stove in the living room and those rooms were only opened when company came. We were comfortable in the large kitchen, and many a yarn was spun there around the kitchen stove. The tea-kettle was always singing, warm water in the reservoir, what more could one ask for. Hans and his pipe, Sena and her reading and knitting, and Carl and I cracking nuts for tomorrow's cookies.

Five years into this marriage a cousin from Iowa, Viola, was hired to help with milking and general housework. No one could help Sena with spring or fall housecleaning because every magazine, paper, old dresses etc were sorted, aired and added to the already bulging closets. Other items stored on the porch included egg cases, washing machine, tubs, dry sink, storm windows, screens and other miscellaneous things. When it rained and the wind blew from the southwest or west, everything moved into the house until the storm was over.

Shortly after Carl and I were married I took confirmation from Pastor Odahl, the Lutheran pastor who married us. I didn't have to be re-baptized and was told that any children I had would certainly not go to hell if they were baptized as infants. The Baptist pastor's wife told me that any children that I have would go straight to hell if there were baptized as infants. My mother taught my early Christian education to me when we did our missionary work. After we moved to Minnesota, I went with my grandmother and mother to church. I really got caught up in the fire and brimstone meetings. It was considered very sinful to dance or play cards. I had never had that kind of preaching in Saskatchewan when Mom talked more about obeying the ten commandments and the love of God. Then when the Baptist congregation heard about my engagement to Carl "a Lutheran", I was more confused than ever. It took me a few years to get over the confusion. My Baptist affiliation left me and I found peace in being a Lutheran.

When I married Carl I didn't automatically become a citizen of the United States. One had to reside in the country for five years before applying for citizenship. Two witnesses were asked to support me. Einar Larson, an insurance agent, and Claude Dresser, a mortician, were two of Carl's friends of good standing, promised to be my witnesses. Now these two gentlemen made the best of this situation. I was so gullible and believed or took seriously anything or everything they told me. Learning much about the United States government and how it operated was a requirement. I was told that the judge was very strict, especially with Canadians. These two witnesses really teased me.

The day finally arrived when I was to appear before the judge, whom I had learned to fear. He appeared to be kind and asked many questions which all were correctly answered. "Name the three branches of government", was the last question. I answered, "Legislative, Judicial," and my mind went blank. "Congratulations, you are now a citizen of the United States." I could hardly believe my ears, as he shook my hand. Einar and Claude signed the papers and were happy for me. They apologized for the hard time they had given me. Now I could vote at school board meetings also. My first vote on the national presidential ballot was for Franklin Delano Roosevelt.

The summer of 1937 I became pregnant. That summer Carl and I lived in Graves vacant home until after potato picking. We had moved into a one room (11 foot by 20 foot) small house, which made it necessary to purchase a small house for one hundred dollars. It was put on a foundation, replastered, painted and stuccoed and it had a chimney. We made two small rooms out of it and Jim was born at Braham Hospital. When Donald was expected an addition (11 foot by 20 foot) was added on the north side with a cellar to store food. This was a warm home and easy to keep warm. I loved this little house. The addition was made into two bedrooms with a closet. It had just been plastered that day when the November 11 storm hit. So we all lived in the big house, including the sausage man, hired man and Viola. We were snug as a bug in a rug. When the storm abated four days later and snow cleared so we could enter, we were back in our home.

When my daughter Linda was born in 1944 we added electricity to this small house. Around this time Carl and his parents started talking about trading houses. There was a lot of discussion. Hans was diagnosed with prostrate cancer and Sena was crippled with arthritis, so it made sense for them to live in the little house which was easier to care for. Hans died in that house in April 1947. Sena continued to live there until she died in June 1956.

The big house was warmer as storm windows had been added to all nine windows and an oil burner stove was added to the living room. No more hot water bottles or heated jugs to be put in beds to warm them up. The old stone porch was a grand place to ride tricycles and other toys. All birthdays, anniversaries, baptismal, confirmations and various other celebrations were held in the big house and spilled over into the porch. The Stone Porch could sit dozens of people in the spring, summer and fall seasons. It wasn't heated in the winter and thus served as a refrigerator.

The Old Stone Porch

In all Carl and I had four children; James Murley born on March 11,1938, Donald Gene, born March 23, 1940, Linda Mary born march 1, 1944, and Connie Ione born August 5, 1948. James was severely burned on October 4, 1948 at age ten. He recovered nicely. All of my children graduated from Mora High School. James studied one year at the University of Minnesota in veterinarian science. Donald attended Gustavus Adolphus Collage studying aeronautical engineering. Linda became a laboratory and x-ray technician. Connie became a beautician.

In 1957 Jim was married to Betty Ritter in August. Just

before the wedding our foreign exchange student, Raili arrived from Finland. In October that year, Donald was killed at age seventeen in a car accident on his way back to Gustavus Adolphus Collage. We had celebrated our twenty-fifth wedding anniversary in July—all of this in a year. When Raili left for her home in Finland in June the following year, we were down to four: Carl, Linda, Connie and I. Linda graduated from high school in 1961 and married Ron Roholt in 1964. Connie and I graduated from high school in June 1966. After Connie married Arden Krinke, Carl and I were alone for several years, not counting Olee the cat and Sparky the dog.

Teaching Sunday school for over fifteen years, singing in church choirs and playing the piano had really been life saving to me. I have a keen interest in birds, conservation, wildlife refuge and rock hunting. All of which have kept me from becoming bored and added a lot of variety to my life. I also was a seamstress—sewing for others and family and altering clothing for the local department store. I had become a volunteer 4-H Club leader in 1947 when Jim became of age. Working with youth has been fulfilling and rewarding.

After Donald's tragic death, I endured one surgery after another. In November of 1960, before Thanksgiving, I was hospitalized with Angina Pictoris. Just before Christmas I became afflicted with acute rheumatoid arthritis. In all, the hospital stay lasted until after Valentines Day in February. I imaging some of you are thinking "what a long time". . . and it was . . . especially the first twenty four days. "She's going to make it", the doctor told Carl.

Excluding family, who do you think my first visitors were?" Of course the Brunswick Livewires 4-H Club leaders. We wrote and planned the Share-the-fun program for our club. That year we did Mother Goose rhymes . . . assigned and wrote speaking parts and singing parts and costume making. This, of course, took many visits as visiting time was limited.

My stay at the hospital was a great learning experience for my 4-H daughters Linda and Connie. They laundered, ironed, baked and cooked. Their 4-H records were full and excellent. At Christmas time Connie put up a small tree and decorated it for my room. She also sang for all the patients. She inherited Carl's strong voice.

Linda was a senior in high school. After I came home from the hospital we planned her graduation. We made a blue and beige woolen lined coat . . . Linda shopped and selected her pattern and material. She even gave a demonstration at the county fair on planning her wardrobe and modeling. I sewed and she pressed. There were four buttons on the coat which cost the high price of fifty cents each . . . they had to compliment the coat, you know . . . and it really turned out beautiful. Her dress was blue flowered embroidered material with inch wide hemstitched line through it, which she strung blue ribbon through. (This offered a real project meeting each day, when possible). Linda played the flute and piccolo in the band and in a trio, so trying on and fitting had to be done when she was available. She also wore this dress for the prom. Our 4-H sewing bulletin was put to good use.

Due to this illness of mine, I ventured into sewing, mending and altering for the clothing store in Mora. Driving tractor and milking cows came to an end for me. My sewing eventually expanded to drapery and refinishing furniture. My "College books" or shall I say "bulletins" came from the Extension office, free. There were many clothing projects held at our home as I got stronger. Whenever the girls had to rip out a poorly sewn seam, I insisted they clap their hands and laugh instead of feeling bad about making a mistake. My daughters did well in their sewing project.

While I was hospitalized the band director visited me often. I was the secretary for the P.T.A. and Linda was student director. He said they were dedicating "I Ain't Done Yet", performed by the band at the band concert to me. Every time I hear that song, or "Seventy-six Trombones" I can see myself in that hospital room, receiving the best of care, learning to walk and being encouraged to play the organ . . . a hymn that the nurses would sing at the beginning of each day.

Now as I continue to learn and teach the 4-H way, I know "I'm not done yet". I wonder if I'll ever graduate from 4-H college . . . maybe I have and don't even realize it!

Hilda in 1948

I have been blessed with eight grandchildren and two step-grandchildren: Jamie, Jeffery, Joel, Beth, Lara, Ross, Todd, Lisa, Christine, and Michael. In turn they have doubly blessed me with great-grandchildren: Mandy, Jason, Mathew, Nicki, Brendan, AJ, and Wolfgang.

Jamie was our first born grandchild. There is something very special about a first born, whether a child, a grandchild or a great-grand child. I remember the day she were born. What a dolly she was. I also remember the day she was baptized. Jamie was only a few weeks old when Betty went back to finish her nurses training and left her with me. I was so glad to be able to do it. Jamie was so loved. It was a sad day when Jim and Betty left he farm to live in Minneapolis; we just didn't see Jamie everyday anymore. Before I knew it Jamie drove her car, a Pontiac I think to visit Carl and I. When I was caring for Jamie I wrote this poem:

> *MY "MISSY"*
>
> *There is no other I remember as so sweet,*
> *When through the snow to grandmas house*
> *You would run in your bare feet*
> *Those days are gone, but memories linger on*
> *They will be forever in my heart, where they belong*
> *You were too small to remember all those times*
> *But before this dear one, was the first smile*
> *The first tooth and then the first step*
> *The old blue buggy where you slept*
> *The bright colored pieces of cloth*
> *Which made you laugh alot*
> *The visits to the neighbors*
> *Where I showed off my live dolly*
> *The Ladies in Aide meetings, you were so jolly*
> *The best thing of all when I dressed you so pretty*
> *You smiled at the camera for a two o'clock sitting*
> *Where the photographer squeaked that cute little kitten*
> *That blue dress was made of scraps by other forsaken*
> *And no one but me knows that your picture was taken.*

Over the years I developed many and diverse ways to baby-sit and entertain grandchildren. As a grandmother anxiously waiting for four to arrive from Minneapolis, I would plan what the children could to do to avoid becoming bored. The old stone porch was a boon for the children. There was everything imaginable on it to play with. No matter what the weather the stone porch was always available.

It was early July and Jim was bringing his four children to the farm to spend a couple of weeks. Grandma was overjoyed whenever they came to visit. Grandpa never got too excited. However, he sat in the lawn chair watching for them. "Here they come," said Grandpa, "fasten everything down!"

"Look at how they've grown since we last saw them." Jamie was eight, Jeff seven, Joel six, and Beth was three. Jamie and Joel had their birthdays on the same day July seventeenth. They sprang out of the car scattering out all over the yard and buildings. Jeff, quick as a monkey, was up in the pine tree, where he loved to sit and watch the world go by. "Bring your suit cases and bags in," their dad suggested, "and put your things away."

After the suitcases and bags had been emptied into the closets and dresser drawers in the rooms that they would be sleeping in upstairs they hurried downstairs chattering like magpies. It was nearly five o'clock and suppertime was always at 5:30 sharp. "Are we going to have pancakes?" asked Jeffery. "Yes, we are because I know how you all love pancakes, especially with fresh strawberries and cream", answered Grandma. "While I make the pancakes will you all please set the table, you always do it so nicely." "How is your sore leg, Grandma?" asked Jamie. "It's much better than what it was, and it hurts less when I'm not on it so much."

"Just smell those pancakes frying makes me so hungry, I think I'll eat a dozen", Joel said. He did get a word in once in a while. He was the quieter of the two boys. As soon as supper was over the two boys rushed to the barnyard. With the help of the dog, they got all the cows in while Grandpa got the milker, strainer and cans ready. "Grandpa, how do cows know which stall to go into?" asked Jeff. "Just try and put one out of its stall, it won't budge—they're really not dumb. I'll spray them with fly spray and Jeff and Joel you can give each cow a measure of feed, then they stand real nice while we milk them," said Grandpa.

Jamie and I had done the dishes and swept the kitchen. With Beth tagging along they went to the barn too. "While I feed the calves their milk and hay, you can give the cats some milk Jamie," I said. "Do they ever like milk!" she said. "Everything on the farm likes milk; doesn't it smell sweet?" "Yes it does," answered Grandma, "in the morning we'll take a gallon up to the house and pasteurize it before we drink it, now its called raw milk. After it's pasteurized then you can drink all you want."

"Why do we have to wash the cows teats?" the boys asked. "Because there's dust and dirt on them. We must have very clean milk so we can realize the best price. The men at the creamery strain and test the milk again so it's a real prize when I get the top pay for our milk," said Grandpa. "There's disinfectant in that teat water so many germs are killed too." Grandpa put the milkers on and as soon as he empties the milk into pails, the boys emptied them into the strainers on the milk cans. They enjoyed doing chores and looked forward to it every day.

"Let's play ball when the chores are done," asked Joel. Everyone agreed. It took no time at all to select the bases. The pine tree was first base, the elm tree second base, the light pole third base, and the clothesline pole passed as home plate. "Beth can't play, she's too little", said Jeff. "She sure can—she runs fast. She does not have to hit or catch the ball either," said Grandpa.

That hour went fast and Beth got to run around the bases a couple of times. She was laughing so hard that last time that she fell down a couple of times and Grandpa pretended he couldn't catch her. The mosquitoes were starting to bite fiercely so all decided to go indoors. Everyone, except Grandpa, got washed up and into their pajamas and sat around the kitchen table for sugar cookies and milk.

Nobody grumbled about going upstairs as they knew I would read to them. She sat in the big rocking chair, (one of Grandma Hanson's), with Beth and Joel on her lap. "What book are you going to read?" asked Jamie. "Have you ever read about the *Five Little Peppers and How They Grew?*" I asked. "Is that about pepper plants, or was their name Pepper?" asked Joel. "Their name was Pepper, just like yours is Ericksen," I answered. "If we read a couple chapters or more each night, we'll probably finish it while you are here." The children loved to hear me read to them. They were in their beds—the boys sitting up in theirs. Jamie was in the single bed. Joel had to look at the quilt on their bed, "Something looks familiar." "Don't you see", said Jamie, "it's pieces put together of all the clothes Grandma made for us, it's just beautiful, so is this one on my bed." You all have a quilt on your bed that I made for you last year", said Grandma.

They were all so attentive as she read during the first chapter, then I suggested they say their prayers—as two of them were looking sleepy. They all folded their hands and prayed, "Now I lay me down to sleep, I pray the Lord my soul to keep. If I should die before I wake, I pray the Lord my soul to take." "What are we going to do tomorrow?" Jamie asked. "If the weather is nice we could go rock hunting in the gravel pit," she said. "Yippee! That would be fun", they all chimed in. "Can we take a lunch along?" After they were all kissed, hugged and tucked in, I started reading Chapter Two. About half way through Beth was asleep, Joel yawned and rolled over saying, "I can't wait until tomorrow, but keep on reading Grandma". When the chapter was finished Jamie

---

111

was the only one awake. I carried Beth to her crib and quietly went downstairs to prepare for rock hunting tomorrow.

Another way I found to entertain the grandchildren was to make up stories. I've included a couple of the stories I have written over the years at the end of this book.

AFTER THE FARM

I know how it feels
Just hanging by a thread
Waiting for some spider
To spin me in its web
But how long must I dangle
So high up in the air
Wondering when the time will come
Yet pretending I don't care
What I need is someone else
To tell me I'll be fine
And maybe let me know
That he would like to intertwine
His life along with mine

Carl and I had fifty-two years of wedded life on the farm. The little house got rented out–the livestock sold–the land rented out. We both had heart troubles and Carl died in July 1984. In all these years I can't remember ever sleeping alone (unless hospitalized) until Carl died. I had slept with mother, Dan and Rudy, Florence, Carl and was now alone.

I stayed two years longer trying to decide whether to live there alone or move in with Connie and her children. I encouraged Viola and Kenny to move to Minnesota to no avail. Jim and Karen thought about coming to the farm and commuting to work but that didn't happen.

113

The roots were deep at the farm and for many years I struggled with that decision. The Stone Porch has weathered many an icy blast; little children occasionally still play house, secretary and doctor nurse in it. The meat barrel, egg cases, and seed corn hung up to dry have all been replaced by refrigerators, purchased egg and seed corn salesmen. Stone Porch Ericksens started with three, swelled to ten, four are at eternal rest. Two families which left one middle-aged tired and worn second generation grandmother and one calico cat. The Stone Porch still remains although the Stone Porch Ericksens no longer enjoy The Porch. The home has been replaced by a younger generation. Three young boys play there now. Overflow parties probably still spill out onto the porch.

The highway in front of the house has been rebuilt at least a half dozen times since the Stone Porch. Each time the road got closer to the porch. The mailbox has been on both sides of the road and even temporarily in the driveway. The number on the box changed numbers from 16 to 28 to 116 to 195—presently it's 325. The Stone porch was "glassed in" in the early sixties so that the three remaining dwellers could hear each other talk because of the highway noise. The pine trees on the lawn, which are younger than the Porch, reach out their branches to nearly touch the familiar, stable, uncracked Stone Porch. They seem to whisper and sigh in the twilight hours as if to say, "You'll be there in the morning for many years to come, dear old Stone Porch."

Connie and the children, Todd and Lisa, begged me to live with them in Elk River. I'm not an alone person so I decided to move to Elk River fifty miles away. I later sold ten acres with the farm buildings. We all lived in a beautiful rambler on the Mississippi River. This truly was a lovely home and yard. I put up the down payment and had a large bedroom on the southeast side with my own bathroom. It was sunny and warm where I sewed on my sewing machine, wrote stories and rocked in my chair.

MY ROOM

In my room, in my room
Many things do happen in my room
Flowers bloom and kittens play
Everything is on display
Books and quilts in disarray
In my room

In my room, in my room
Sun in shining, there's no gloom
There I sit and sew on cotton
As my chair is gently rocking
Sorry, lonesomeness forgotten
In my room

In my room, in my room
"Prairie Winds" are written down
In my room
As I pause, and start to thinking
And my eyes with tears are blinking
My old friends and home are missing
In my room

I felt transplanted for a long time but got settled in by joining Central Lutheran Church, Mary Circle, the choir, and started the River City Kids 4-H club. On December 5 or 7, 1987 I had quadruple bypass heart surgery. In January on the bypasses plugged so I had to have an angioplasty. In all I was in the hospital forty-three days. A second quadruple bypass heart surgery was performed on March 3, 1997. After this surgery I spent twenty days in a nursing home. In August the same year I had a brain hemorrhage and spent another twenty days in another nursing home. I guess I'm a survivor. Regular trips to the doctor and medications now are a costly and permanent part of my life.

Sitting quietly in a rocking chair, reading or singing to all of my grandchildren had been such a joy. Some of the great grandchildren are too big to hold—but regardless how big they are they can be hugged and kissed. As the grandchildren and great grandchildren got older, rocking and holding has been replaced by making quilts and afghans for all of them. I'm still making patch quilts and sewing and making gifts.

From time to time I like to reflect on things that were common or not so common a half a century or more ago. One time lately as I was sitting in the car in a grocery parking lot I watched things in the carts that would have been absolutely strange to me in the 1920s, 30s, or 40s. The bottom shelf of one cart was jammed with cases of pop. The top bin was full of a combination of paper products such as paper napkins, paper towels, Kleenex, bathroom tissue, Kotex and diapers. I wondered "What did these things costs?"

When I was a girl and up until my last child was born, all these things were foreign to me. Flour, sugar and salt all came in cloth containers. These containers, or sacks, were all washed and soaked in strong soap to remove all the printing. Diapers, underwear, skirts and blouses were made from flour sacks, including sheets, pillow cases and dresser scarves. Handkerchiefs were made from the smaller bags. Evenings were spent pulling thread to straighten the material. It took five hundred pound flour sacks to make a sheet. When feed for the animals came in colored and figured sacks they made lovely clothing and luncheon cloths. It was fun to go to the creamery, where feed was sold and pick out several bags that were alike to make clothing our of. Four dozen cloth diapers lasted to diaper my first three children.

New Curity diapers were given for Connie's baby shower. These were not square shaped. They were oblong and folded triple. These were so nice and soft compared to the flannel and sack ones used earlier. None of these were thrown away when they were no longer used as diapers. They made lovely towels especially for window cleaning, no lint dust cloths, so many uses. Cloth rags used before Kotex, were soaked, washed and used over and over again months after month, anyone remember?

There also was very little garbage back then. Nearly all our food came in jars. Vegetables, fruit, beef, pork, chicken was all home canned. Homemakers were kept busy preparing food that was boiled in hot water bath for hours on a wood burning stove. Meats were canned in the late fall or early winter, vegetables and fruit in the summer. It did not take long to make a meal in the busy planting or haying season; just open a jar of meat (beef, pork, or chicken), a jar of vegetables, a jar of fruit, and homemade bread and butter made everyone content. These glass jars of food looked so nice stored on shelves in the cellar, where potatoes, carrots and onions were also stored in bins.

I still can apples and make jam, also beet and cucumber pickles. The freezer holds a good supply of corn, squash and rhubarb. Of course, going along with "PROGRESS" we, Connie and I, use paper towels, napkins, Kleenex and other paper products; but it all takes money which we had little of a half century or more ago.

PEANUT BUTTER CLUSTERS
1 cup white Karo syrup
1 cup sugar
Bring above ingredients to a boil, Remove from heat and add 1 and 1/2 cup
crunchy peanut butter and 6 and 1/2 cups of Rice Krispies. Drop from spoon
onto waxed paper.

During the first forty-two years as a 4-H Adult leader, I received the W.C.C.O. Good Neighbor Award. I was named the volunteer of the week in the spring of 1996. I received a diploma for writing. I'm proud of that accomplishment. In November 1997 I was given a grand party at Central Lutheran Church for fifty years as a 4-H volunteer leader. Meeting former county agents and 4-H'ers was such a thrill. The fifty big red roses in a crystal vase were the gift from my club the "River City Kids" and brought many tears.

My dream at sixteen to become a math teacher has somewhat been fulfilled by teaching youth to grow in learning and sharing their leadership skills and to stay on the straight and narrow road, has been rewarding. I still enjoy 4-H meetings in this my fifty-second year as a leader. I can still contribute something—especially praising and giving love and encouragement to youth to do their best and that's all any of us can do.

"The children of today love luxury, they have bad manners, contempt for authority, they show disrespect for elders and love to chatter in place of exercise".

One might think the above was written by someone today who had forgotten his childhood. It was actually written by Socrates back in the days before Christ, sometime between 469 and 399 B.C.

Does this really describe youth? Is that what we are coming to? My personal foresight of 4-H youth in the future is stated in three visions—loyalty, education and discrimination. Loyalty is being faithful to a cause, ideal or occupation. 4-H teaches youth to be loyal to our home, club, community, country, church and world instead of luxury, bad manners or contempt for authority. We as 4-Hers, young or old, learn respect for not only ourselves but for people, such as club leaders, extension, teachers and those around us. We have been taught to set goals and establish responsibilities for our thoughts, words and deeds.

My vision for 4-H in the future is we will have even greater power–in more than fifty nations of the world we have young people belonging to organizations very much like our 4-H philosophy. It is obvious that 4-H has given us the strength and morality to be loyal to our lives and organizations and the people and things within it. In Minnesota alone, there are over 138,000 youth involved in 4-H nationally. What a power we will have in elections alone when youth become of voting age.

That brings up the vision of education. It is imperative that youth get as much education as they can afford. In matters that concern them most is alcohol and drug abuse. There would be no drug problems if no one misused and abused drugs. Drug pushers would have no customers. Smugglers would have no money. The lives of millions of people would be saved. How does this problem affect you and I? My friends may try to persuade me to take some. You may think to yourself, "I don't want to be left out of the crowd. I don't want tot be considered a chicken or a sissy". You may have so many problems at school, home or work that you would take anything just to feel good again. But, STOP and THINK again— it takes much more guts to say "NO" and you can be so proud of yourself that you had the strength and courage to keep clean.

We can fight this desire by learning as much as possible about our body and mind—education, being able to talk to a trusted adult, or an understanding parent will really help you if one has a problem. If you want to live a long life and keep your body clean, think twice, maybe three times before giving in to someone who makes fun of you because you haven't got drunk, high on drugs, fill your lungs full of smoke, or succumb to a teenage pregnancy. Education and heeding it is the key.

In Minnesota 4-Hers are addressing the drinking and driving problem using SADD, MADD and affected individuals and sheriffs as resources. With the information they have gathered they have set up booths at County Fairs and prepared flyers for the press when politicians visit to their area. Helping conduct workshops shows that youth can do and help prevent the use of all these destructive things. Our youth will also have to face the issues of conservation, acid rain, water shed, soil erosion, pollution, garbage and on and on it goes. 4-Hers can learn much about this by taking on projects that pertain to these issues. Future 4-Hers will be better informed than we are today. They will be educated, informed and will do a super job in these issues.

Discrimination. 4-Hers, families and leaders do not discriminate. We believe that everyone regardless of the color of their skin, their religion or politics, short, tall, skinny or heavy, have equal rights to enjoy the freedoms of this land. No two people are the same. No two children in a family are the same. No one motivator is going to work with all of them. How can one determine what motivates us? Ask yourself some of these questions. What motivates us? What are some of the things that we do that makes us feel good? What are some of the things that make us feel sad or bad? Do we like to spend our time relaxing? Socializing? Reading? Playing? What can we do about apathy?

It takes negotiation. Willing to work together can resolve most problems. It is important to give as well as to get. Community activities create interest and motivation such as the Community Festival, County Fairs, Community Pride, Share the Fun, public speaking, and camps. Having basic goals and guidelines that might be a bit different from those of a usual 4-H group. For example, plan a car wash as a fundraiser. Let the kids do as much of the planning as possible. Having responsibility helps them feel good about themselves and helps them grow as individuals. Then have a cook out as a reward. When members come up with activities of their own, they become more enthusiastic about activities they chose themselves.

Youth have so much energy, it seems their batteries never need recharging. 4-Hers guided by adult leaders can and will make this a better world if given the opportunity to motivate others to avoid drugs and alcohol, obey laws, and respect those in authority. It is such a joy for me to watch and listen as parents, leaders and 4-H members get ready for the fair. There is so much enthusiasm as children and parents work together preparing exhibits, making banners and building floats. No one is left out, everyone is interested in what each one is bringing to the fair and complimenting each for reaching the goals set by the club. The parents in this club are so willing and encouraging their young children to think of others. What they can give is truly so encouraging as I look into the future that all will be well.

THE 4-H PLEDGE
I pledge my HEAD to clearer thinking-
My HEART to greater loyalty-
My HANDS to larger service-
My HEALTH to better living
for my family, my club, my community and my world.

The home on the river in Elk River, too, did not last. When Connie had to start hiring to get the large lawn moved and snow shoveled it was put up for sale and sold immediately before the town house was completed. I lived a month with Tom and Vicki having my own bedroom and bath, very nice. They became dear friends.

Presently I am living in a Meadow Lark town house with Connie and her new husband, Harlan. I like the neighborhood and have friends right here a few steps away. Which of all these homes would I say I was the happiest? It would be a close draw between the big square house on the farm or that little house. There is something great and warm about that smaller home, it takes less money to heat, furnish and much less time to keep spotless.

EPILOGUE

I am just a plain, ordinary, conservative person. My love of God and country has been strong with a keen interest in County, State, National, and World Affairs. There never was a struggle for power or the limelight. I was taught early in life to respect those in authority, love of country and respect for the flag. The Ten Commandments were to be lived by daily. Naughty words and swearing was washed out of the mouth with soap. I was so thankful and blessed for having a very loving Christian mother and a strict father. It is to their credit I grew up to be the honest and hard working citizen that I am. I can truthfully say that the beatitudes were the framework of my life. In my early youth, the 4-H pledge shared that framework.

Accepting Christ as my Savior and being able to witness and share my faith by sharing my talents as a Sunday Day teacher, singing in choirs, shaping a loaf of bread, sewing on a button, or tying quilts. I hope and pray that I have left an indelible way of life for my children, grandchildren and great-grandchildren.

I can go to my heavenly home with peace of mind knowing that no one can say they saw me drunk, I was not caught stealing or nor did I take anyone's life. I have rubbed elbows with "The Cream of the Crop" in both adults and youth via Church and 4-H. That "Little Light of Mine", I am still going to let it shine and "Brighten the Corner" wherever I am.

PRAIRIE WINDS
Have you really seen the wind
Could you ever prove its there
I see it in the waving prairie grass
And the many puffy clouds that pass
Today my laundry waved at me
As leaves were rustling in the trees
Wind has no color, sex or creed
But I can hear it in the weeds
It's unseen-something using space
Now it's caressing my hair and face
So much like God–its everywhere

c

SHORT STORIES

THE THIEVES

Twiggy Bird was a dear friend of Mother Rabbit. She flew in every day with the news of the day. The coffeepot was always on so the two of them would chat away as they had their coffee. One day in autumn Twiggy Bird arrived with this news: "Mother Rabbit, I know where there are some delicious pie apples." "Please tell me where they are, I need to make two pies for the social tonight," answered Mother Rabbit. "They are at Rascal Sam Rabbit's wood shed, I saw him stealing them off of Mr. and Mrs. Snoopy Rabbit's tree," answered Twiggy Bird. "Will you help me get them?" asked Mother Rabbit. "Oh yes," replied Twiggy Bird, "let's go right now while Rascal Sam Rabbit is raiding Mamie Mouse's carrot patch."

Mother Rabbit picked up two grocery bags and they left for the woodshed. Twiggy Bird flew ahead singing all the way. When they passed Mamie Mouse's house, she was so curious seeing Mother Rabbit's grocery bags, that she instantly dropped her apron and started to follow after her. Twiggy Bird and Mother Rabbit found the apples. They soon had the bags full and were on their way back. "I'll stay and help you pare the apples while you prepare the crusts," offered Twiggy Bird. "Thank you so much," replied Mother Rabbit, "that way we will get done sooner. I hope we have enough apples to make and extra apple pie to have with our coffee." They both got real busy pealing apples and rolling out pie crusts. They could almost taste how good the pies would be.

In the meantime Rascal Sam Rabbit came carrying the carrots to store in his woodshed. As he looked in he saw his apples were gone. "What in the world happened to my apples?" He was so excited and angry he paced the floor. As he rounded one corner he spied Mamie Mouse. "What are you doing here?" he yelled. "Did you eat all my apples? I hope you get a real good stomach ache," he continued.

"No! No! I didn't eat your apples", Mamie Mouse replied trembling, "but I know where they are. Mother Rabbit and Twiggy Bird took them. They need them to make pies for the social tonight." "Thanks for telling me," grumbled Rascal Sam Rabbit. "I have other plans for tonight, like eating pie. Mother Rabbit makes such good pies." In due time Mother Rabbit had three pies cooling on the windowsill. She put the coffee pot on and Twiggy Bird flew out and sat in the tree. After a few minutes Twiggy spied Rascal Sam Rabbit sneaking up the back path to Mother Rabbit's house. She knew he was up to mischief so she started yelling "mother Rabbit! Mother Rabbit!" She had hardly got he words out when Rascal Sam Rabbit snatched a pie and was gone in an instant. Mamie Mouse and Mr. and Mrs. Snoopy Rabbit heard Twiggy Bird screaming and hurriedly arrived to see hat the excitement was all about. Peeking in the door they saw Mother Rabbit throw up her arms in dismay. "There goes Rascal Sam Rabbit with one of my pies. Now we can't have pie with our coffee. I am so disappointed."

Mamie Mouse arrived just in time to hear Mr. and Mrs. Snoopy Rabbit say, "She deserved to lose that pie, because she stole those apples." "I don't think so," squeaked Mamie Mouse, "she did all that work making those pies."

A BIRTHDAY SURPRISE

Tony is an active, slight little boy, with an imagination that sometimes runs wild. His dark brown eyes search yours for the love and understanding he expects from you. Being sentimental and tender hearted; he demonstrates warmth for people, especially his grandmother, which endears him to all. Disappointments can fill his eyes with tears that spill out all over his face—finally breaking into sobs. Happiness otherwise can explode into "yippee", or "Let's do it right away. I can't wait grandma, not a minute."

At grandma's suggestion, Tony finds the alphabet book she had given him the previous year when he started nursery school. By now he could identify the letters and recognize most of the pictures. "I'm five now", he commented. "In September I start Kindergarten." "Do you think that you will like to go to school every day?" grandma asks. "You have a very good memory, Tony. As you grow older you will have many more things to remember." "Say, grandma do you think an elephant ever gets filled up? They must be hungry all the time," he mused as he turned the pages. "Here's a "P" what king of a bird is this?"

"That is a parrot" grandma answered. "It is a tropical bird with brilliant plumage: they can talk and repeat nearly everything you say." "You mean I could talk to it?" Tony inquired, and in the next breath exclaimed, "Could I have one? I could keep it in a cage just like this one in the picture and we have crackers. Could I, grandma?" he pleaded. "I cannot answer that question, Tony, because that decision has to be made by your parents. A parrot would be a big responsibility for you. Parrots make a mess like a chicken, they also lose their feathers. I am sure your mommy will not accept that. Go ask her and get her opinion. She is in the garden." "Okay, I'll go right out and ask her. Maybe I can have one for my birthday." For the moment the alphabet book was forgotten along with hunting agates. Now grandma had warned him about mommy not going along with his desire of getting a parrot so Tony has to work up enough courage to ask his mother. She answered his question with dismay.

"A parrot!" exclaimed his mother, "wherever did you get an idea like that?" "Grandma was reading my alphabet book to me and there's a picture in it of a parrot in a cage. It would be a neat thing to give me for my birthday. I could give it a name and feed him, oh mommy, could I please have a parrot for my birthday?" he sobbed. "Parrots are colorful", she continued, " but they are messy with crackers all over the carpeting. They could get lousy. They are very squawky. I don't think that would be wise. Your dad would have no part of it, besides, parrots cost a lot of money. You better suggest something else for your birthday. Last year you asked for a hammer. Remember how you accidentally broke the glass in the door. You always ask for such grown up things, although, I have to admit you did real well with the watering can when you helped me with my plants. How about a cute kitten or something to ride on like Big Wheels?"

Her suggestion did not spark any desire for either one in spite of the child being easy to please. Mommy had suggested some nice things for his birthday but Tony just could not get a parrot out of his mind. He even talked about it to God that night as daddy listened to his prayers. The days went by into weeks, then months. Tony mentioned the parrot continually. He had an elephant memory where that parrot was concerned. Finally the morning of his birthday arrived. He awoke to the most beautiful whistling and something saying "Good Morning, pretty boy."

Tony's big brown eyes opened instantly and there by his window he saw a cage. "I don't believe it," he said as he sprang out of bed and rushed over to the cage. He saw a beautiful yellow and blue-green bird looking right at him and

c

saying repeatedly, "Good morning, pretty boy, good morning, pretty boy." "Oh, you pretty bird," Tony exclaimed, as he turned and bounded up the stairs to his parents' bedroom. "It is beautiful daddy and it talks too, mommy. What kind of bird is it?" He was so excited.

"That is a parakeet, Tony, grandma suggested it to me. It belongs to the parrot family. In fact it is a small parrot wit a long tail. This little bird will make a wonderful pet and is easier to care for. Its name starts with a "P" like parrot. You could call it Peetie." "Thank you, thank you, mommy and daddy." He was so elated. After kissing them both he hurried to show his birthday present to his sister who was already awakened by all the talking. He just loved it. It really was a parrot, a small one, but he didn't care. His birthday wish was granted.

LADYBUG FLY AWAY HOME

One warm sunny Saturday in September, Danny aged eight, and his mother an arthritic, had been picking vegetables in the garden. Fresh carrots and ripe, red tomatoes were a special favorite of Danny's. He didn't object to making the last trip to the garden to pick tomatoes. Their basket was nearly full and both of them were getting tired. Then Danny noticed some bugs on the tomato plants.

What kind of bugs are these, Mom?" asked Danny. "Do we kill them?" "No, no, we don't kill these bugs", answered Mom. " call them good luck bugs. Their correct name is Ladybug or Ladybird. Sit down beside me and I'll tell you something about Ladybugs." Danny was quite surprised to see his mother pick up several of the bugs and let them crawl on her hands and around through her fingers. "Take a good look at them," she said. "Hold some in your hand. They won't hurt you. See how bright colored they are. Most Ladybugs are red or yellow with a varying number of black or white spots on their backs. These are red with black spots. Ladybugs are really small beetles. There are about 2000 species of them. They can also fly. Some species are not beneficial.

"Their bodies are kind of circular," commented Danny. "They aren't very big. This one is about the size of a pea. Look at its eyes. It has a mouth and two antennae on its head. Are all Ladybugs this size?" he asked. "No, Ladybugs vary in size," answered mom. She moved to a more comfortable position. The ground was hard for her to sit upon. "The smallest is 1/25 of an inch long and the largest, found in Southern Asia is 1/2 inch long. Ladybugs are found all over the world. They were imported to the United States from Australia and were credited by practically wiping out the cottony cushion scale which was destroying the citrus crop in California."

"How come you know so much about Ladybugs?" asked Danny. "Because I was interested in them and did some research on them," answered his mother. "They are harmless, friendly, pretty and beneficial to man. I like to see them in the garden, something like soldiers protecting our plants. These little beetles lay yellow eggs in batches. The hatched eggs are larvae or small caterpillars. Larvae bodies are elongated, soft, segmented and covered with hairlike spines. Ladybugs and their larvae live on harmful insects such as aphids, mites, mealy bugs, plant lice and others. The harmful insects destroy potato, tomato and citrus crops. Crops are saved by these active Ladybugs."

"Where do they go in the winter?" questioned Danny. "The adults hibernate in enormous numbers on the high mountains. In the early spring they are collected and distributed among fruit, potato and tomato growers. Seed catalogs have them for sale. They can be purchased by the pint or quart. There are about 5,000 in a half pint which sells for over $8.50. Ladybugs love people and devour insects, re-member that," said Mom. "I read in a book, just recently, that the "Lady" portion of the name supposedly dates back to the Middle Ages when they were dedicated to the Virgin. Later they were granted a small measure of immortality thor-ough the couplet "Ladybug, Ladybug, fly away home. Your house is on fire and your children will burn."

"That sounds like a nursery rhyme," chuckled Danny. "Let's call it a day. I would really like to have a tomato and some crisp carrots to eat." "Okay", agreed his mother, "but I'm going to take a few of these Ladybugs along to the house and let them search through my houseplants. They might find some kind of bad insect on that droopy violet of mine."

WHO'S SLEEPING IN MY BED?

It was in late October last fall that Johnny, age ten, had joined the rural neighborhood 4-H club. He had begged to join the previous year taking a sheep project but his parents told him he was too young for that project. He had watched sheep judging that year at the county fair and was determined to have a lamb. They were convinced that in a year Johnny would be interested in some other project. They were dairy farmers and why couldn't he take a calf project?

Now Johnny was a year older and had enrolled in the sheep project. He had read the sheep bulletin from cover to cover. A pen had been made in a draft-free corner of the barn. Milk, grain, hay, everything he needed, was available but his dad wasn't a sheep man. That meant that he would have to buy a lamb. Most sheep men wouldn't sell ewe lambs. Johnny definitely wanted a ewe lamb. This created a problem. "I'll just have to hope that someone will have a bottle lamb to sell to me," said Johnny.

January and February went by. Then one night late March, Johnny 's dad was reading the weekly advertiser. "Johnny come here", he said. He came wondering what dad wanted. "Here's an ad offering bottle lambs for sale. Do you still want a lamb?" "I do, I do", answered Johnny, "call that number right away before they're all gone." He was so excited he was jumping up and down. His dad dialed the number. The phone rang many times. No one answered. "We'll try again around eight," his dad said. Johnny felt a little downhearted. He kept checking the clock. The time went so slow. Every five minutes seemed endless. His dad broke the silence by asking, "Providing you can get a lamb, how do you plan to pay for it?"

"I've saved five dollars, Dad," answered Johnny. "My 4-H leader said that in most cases parents buy the first animal. Then they keep the first offspring." "I don't intent to raise sheep," said Dad. "I've got enough to do with dairy cattle." "I can help you more with the chores and the yard, Dad. Grandma said she'd pay me for mowing her lawn. I'll pay you back, honest, I will." "All right", replied Dad, "lets try that number again." Still there was no answer. "Finish your homework, Johnny, I'll call in the morning."

Johnny finished his homework and went to bed early. He laid there thinking and wondering if the lamb would have a white or black face. It didn't matter to him, just so it was a ewe lamb. He woke early the next morning. He could hardly wait until that phone call was made. Dad dialed the number. "Hello Nelsons, do you have any bottle lambs left? You do! Good. Johnny and I will be right over." They got in the pickup and off they went to the Nelson's farm. Mrs. Nelson met them in the yard and led the way to the sheep barn. "There isn't any choice left", she said. "The smallest triplet is left. I had twelve bottle lambs and I wouldn't sell this one if I weren't so tired of bottle feeding lambs three times a day. This ewe lamb is a month old. Johnny can have it for twenty-five dollars. Don't feed it too much. Let it be a little hungry each time you feed it. If it gets too much, it could get sick."

Johnny's dad paid Mrs. Nelson for the lamb. He carried the lamb to the pick-up. It stood on the seat between them on the way home. "B-a-a-a B-a-a-ah", bleated the lamb. "Don't cry ", said Johnny, as he patted her head. "You'll soon be home in your own pen. You and I will be the best of friends. Please don't get sick, I want you to grow fast." He was so happy that tears spilled down his cheeks. Johnny laughed as he watched the lamb's stub tail wiggle back and forth when it took its bottle. "I wish I could keep her in my bedroom to-night," remarked Johnny at the supper table. "She's lonesome when I leave her."

"You're not bringing that lamb in the house", grumbled Dad, "that's an order". Johnny looked disappointedly at his mother, but said no more. When he was finished eating, he asked to be excused, picked up his dirty dished and placed them near the sink. Out the door he went to be with his lamb. His parents missed him about nine o'clock. "Did you see Johnny come in?" asked Mother. "No, I didn't", answered Dad. "Do you suppose he's still with the lamb?" "Let's go and see," suggested Mother. They walked side by side down to the barn and over to the corner where the pen was. "Will you just look at that," said Dad. "I'm getting the camera and take a picture," answered Mom.

You guessed right. Johnny and his lamb were curled up together sound asleep in the lamb's bedroom. "Looks like we'll be raising sheep too," said Dad. They both were happy that they had purchased the lamb that Johnny had wanted for so long. Now they were all happy.

BE ON TIME

Robert Edstrom, age eight, a chubby second grader, cute, loud, and naughty, taxes all the patience of his Sunday school teacher and disturbs the other classmates consisting of three girls and four boys. He is very bright and an excellent reader. He is the youngest child in his family and has a fourteen year old sister. He dislikes his sister, claiming that she hates him. He told the class that his parents never attend church. His parents are faithful choir members. He likes to be the first one to class and generally is. This particular Sunday he was late and was very upset when he arrived. Robert is mischievous and does most anything to get attention.

"Where is Robert?" asked Abbey. "He is always the first one here, because he likes to get a star by his name." "I do not think we should wait any longer", said Brian, "otherwise we will not get our lesson done before it is Singtime." "Let's not wait any longer, maybe he is sick," agreed Abbey "he is trouble anyway."

"The lesson today is about Children of God, and talks about baptism. The lesson centralizes on the baptism of Jesus, by John the Baptist", announces their teacher. She had made a sign, "Children of God", on bright red paper and pinned it on the bulletin board. She had also made nice paper children joining hands out of white paper and pinned it beneath the "Children of God" sign. The class was in the process of each child writing their name on the cutouts. They had all been baptized and believed they were children of God. The door sprung open and in burst Robert taking off his cap and jacket and tossing them in the corner. He was so upset that he pushed his chair back out three feet from the table and sat there pouting.

"Who was the first one here?" he asked. "Brian was", answered Abbey, "he has been sick all week with an ear in-

c

fection and had tubes put in his ears. We are all happy that he is feeling better." "Who made "The Children of God" sign and the cutouts?" asked Robert. (He didn't like to be called Robert he only answered to Bobby). "Our teacher made the signs", answered Abbey. "Are you going to sign the attendance chart, Bobby?" asked the teacher. He abruptly got up and signed the attendance chart.

"I am not signing "The Children of God" thing though, he said loudly, because I'm a child of the devil." Everyone was amazed and could not take their eyes off of him. By this reaction Bobby crawled under the table and disturbed the class by pulling on their trousers and causing a disturbance. The Superintendent just entered the room to pick up the attendance record and offering. Their teacher asked her "What do I do or how do I go about reporting children who disturb the class?"

"Thank you, if this continues I'll let you know", she answered. The class was now busy filling in the questions and coloring on their four pages of lessons. "What about Bobby, he is still under the table causing me trouble," asked Abbey. "We will just forget about him today, all he wants is attention. If he continues to stay under there the Superintendent will take him down to the office." Bobby crawled out from under the table and proceeded to the bulletin board. He tapped teacher on the shoulder and whispered, "I signed that, "Children of God" sign."

"I knew you would after you gave a lot of thought to what you had said", she smiled. "Can I read the last page about the prayer?" asked Bobby. "Yes, you may," answered the teacher. Bobby was a very good reader. The door opened and a lady said "Singtime". All the papers were gathered up, crayons etc put into the basket. It was neat for the next class.

Singtime was for all the children in grades kindergarten, one and two. The songleader announced that Mrs. Ericksen would play the piano today in the absence of the regular pianist. After several songs were sung, the songleader announced, "I want all the second graders to stand up and sing the next song." All stood up and right in the middle stood Bobby singing his heart out with a big smile on his face.

MY FRIEND TONY TOAD

One spring day Hilda sat down to rest after weeding her petunias in the flower boxes. Suddenly out of the corner of her eye she spied Tony Toad. "Tony, I'm so glad to see you. You are back again after your long winter nap." "I'll always come back here, I like the sun in the morning, It keeps me warm. Then in the afternoon when the sun gets hot, I squat here under the flower boxes and keep cool. Do you ever get warts on your hands? I like it when you pick me up by my backbone and talk to me. You always ask me to sing for you. You are kind to me."

"To answer your question, No I never have had warts. I don't believe that old story about getting warts from holding toads. That's an old untrue myth like using toads for making witches brew. I think you are beautiful Tony." "A lot of people thing toads are physically unattractive. Even though you have a squat, chunky, wart covered sombre colored body, your beautiful eyes have large gold colored irises located so you have a wide range of vision. Oops, I saw you get that fly with your long flexible tongue. Do you like flies?"

"I like flies, slugs, cutworms, aphids and others," Tony answered. "These are harmful to your garden, especially to your lettuce plants. I hop down there every night and get my fill. I like to hunt at night and lay around during the day, especially here in your petunias, where I can dig myself into the soft earth. Sometimes I hop down to the pond behind the barn. I saw a snake there. It didn't see me or else I would have been his dinner." "Promise me that you won't go to the pond again. I'll leave you plenty of water here in this shallow pan. I would love to know where you go in the winter."

"See that hold in the foundation", he answered. "When it starts to get cold, I just wiggle through that crack and bury myself in the dirt where you grow your celery and sleep the time away. I feel very safe there."

HANS

There he is again. It is 6:30 p.m. and he arrives promptly, as usual, to play in the park. He is eight years old, athletic, strong and about four and a half feet tall. His shoulders are wide, his legs straight. He was slightly pigeon-toed. A well-shaped head, held high, is covered with a mop of sun-bleached thick blonde hair. Dark brown eyes lookup at you, as a wide smile exposes gaps amid his small pearly-white teeth. He appears to be slightly overweight. His name is Hans.

Boldly approaching a high fort like structure he shoved his way between the other children. Being the first to reach the top pleases him obviously, because he flaunts his muscular arms and thrusts out his chest. The cement circular culvert is no challenge either. He crawls through this rapidly. He resembles a miniature Tarzan, especially so when he grabs a heavy rope and swings too and fro—yells included.

Having observed this lad several times, one would say without hesitation, that he is noisy active, alert and quite demonstrative. Treating girls as the weaker sex isn't descriptive of him either. This probably is reflective of having three older sisters. He pouts when he is advised to take turns at the swings or teeter-totters. His appearance is definitely of no concern to him. His pants and shirt seldom match. Whether they are patched, worn out at the seat or knees, makes no difference to him—just so the garments have pockets.

He just loves pockets. One day he was displaying all his treasures contained in his pockets. Stones of various sizes and shapes came out of one pocket. Another held a variety of rusty nails, odd sized nuts and bolts and a small broken screwdriver. After all his pockets were emptied there was quite an assortment added to the pile, including pieces of cloth, string, small bottles containing bugs, some alive, an empty zipper container, a Jacques Corn jack-knife, bubble gum, unwrapped candy, and an empty safety match cover. He is in heaven when he visits a junkyard or a run down farm.

This interesting child also enjoys fishing and camping. His love of the outdoors is unbelievable. The coldest blasty day in winter will find him outside romping with a dog or building a snow fort. In the summer time, he resembles a pocket gopher. He digs holes and tunnels continuously in his large natural sandbox. A coffee can near by contains the worms or grubs that he finds–someone might go fishing. His grandpa likes to fish too, and often takes him along. Hans enjoys eating by a campfire. He accepts dehydrated food, too, when hungry enough. Roasted marshmallows are his favorite they go down by the pound.

In spite of Hans being somewhat smartalicy and bratty, he is warm hearted, friendly and affectionate. He loves animals and they love him in return. Hans is very capable and dependable. He is personable, honest and true. In fact, I think I'll approach him and make myself acquainted. In fact, I'll bring my 4-H packet along and invite him to join. I would like to really know him and be his friend.

DANIEL JOINS 4-H

After spending several days with his Aunt Tillie attending the county fair, Daniel could hardly wait to go home. He thought the sheep were just great. While watching the judging of sheep he though to himself-"Now I can do that. I'll get me a lamb and show my friends and sisters that I can show an animal at the fair." While he waited for his parents, he asked Aunt Tillie, "How can I get a lamb and take it to the fair?"

"First of all, you should join a 4-H club to get all the information about sheep", said Aunt Tillie. "It's hard work, but its an experience and education you'll never forget. You will learn to feed, care and keep a record of the costs of a lamb and the feed it eats." "Gosh, I can do that ", boasted Daniel. Just then his parents arrived. Daniel bounded out the screen door, swinging it wide enough to break the chain. He gave his dad a bear hug and his mom a quick kiss. "Hey, you guys, Aunt Tillie took me to the fair everyday. It was really neat. I've got a great idea, too. I was gonna wait 'til we get home to talk about it, but I just can't wait. I wan to talk about sheep business", he said.

"Dad I want a lamb to raise. I want to join a 4-H Club. Aunt Tillie told me all about it. I helped a man feed and water his sheep. He must of had a hundred of them. Sheep have lambs and grow wool all over them. Their meat is called mutton and lamb. I just gotta have a lamb." Daniel was out of breath. "Nonsense," answered his dad, "you have a dog, a cat, and a new bike. Aren't you ever satisfied." "But Dad this is different. I'd like to try this sheep prospect. I also found out that bankers loan money to kids for their animal projects." "That's something your mother and I have to talk about, he said. "I don't want to hear anymore about it now."

Daniel was disappointed at his dad's lack of interest. He went to sulk. He chose to sit in the car. He thought about many things. "Maybe I asked too soon", talking out loud. "But 4-H enrollment is now." He kicked the back of the front seat. After much debating Daniel enrolled in the Busy Beavers 4-H club. His sisters teased him about getting a "Baa Baa". Daniel thoughts bout his sisters were rather sour. "I'll show them a thing or two. All they think about is T.V. and giggling about boys." He thought he was quite smart.

Early in the spring Daniel and his dad attended a sheep auction. He insisted on a Finnish Landruce, noted for multiple births, and their quality of wool. He liked their white faces. Daniel spent many hours training his lamb. He never grumbled. He told his lamb all his troubles. She never talked back. She often rubbed her head against his leg. "I really love you, Woolly", he said. "You're the neatest pet, even when I caught heck when you got into mom's garden. He spent many hours getting Woolly ready for the fair. Getting the straw out of her wool was the hardest. Teaching her to stand in the proper way for the judge was hard too.

He won a red ribbon at the fair. By watching the older 4-H'ers he learned where he made his mistakes. The judge told him he'd done a good job especially so being it was his first time. When he came home after judging his sisters chided him, "Where's your blue ribbon?" "I really didn't want one", he answered. "I learned I was a winner by just trying. You never get anywhere if you don't at least try. Next year I will do better."

Learn by doing.